To, David,

Love from Margaret.

Christmas 1996.

RETURN OF THE
LITTLE VILLAN

RETURN OF THE
LITTLE VILLAN

BRIAN LITTLE

WITH

PETER WHITE

SPORTS PROJECTS

•

First published in Great Britain in 1996 by
SPORTS PROJECTS LTD
188 Lightwoods Hill, Smethwick, Warley, West Midlands B67 5EH

•

ISBN 0 946866 04 X

•

•

A catalogue record for this book is available from the British Library

•

Printed in Great Britain

Contents

Bringing It All Back Home

by Andy Gray

I played alongside some great footballers during my career but I have no hesitation in saying that Brian Little was the most talented of them all.

I had great times at Wolves with John Richards and at Everton with Graeme Sharp. I partnered Kenny Dalglish for Scotland and although Kenny was arguably the best all-round player I have known there was no one to match the natural talent of Brian.

I enjoyed a great playing career in England but if it had not been for the four years I spent alongside Brian then I would not have achieved half the success I managed.

The things he could do with a football were sometimes unbelievable. My game was all about aggression and battling, his was all about skill and subtlety. We complemented one another; sometimes the understanding we had was like telepathy.

But if someone had asked me 15 years ago if I thought Brian would ever make a successful manager my immediate reaction would have been 'No'!

Brian always gave me the impression he was playing the game just because he was so good at it. Nothing was difficult for him. But I always felt that once his playing days were over he would drift away from the game and do something totally different.

Let's face it, nice guys do not usually make good managers,

although there have been exceptions to the rule. I immediately think of people like Bob Paisley and Joe Fagan. Now Brian falls into that category. Maybe the fact that his career ended so prematurely influenced his decision to achieve something else within the game.

Some managers begin their careers right at the top. I am thinking of people like Bryan Robson, Kenny Dalglish and Glenn Hoddle. Brian was different. He began in the lower reaches and served a long apprenticeship. But his single-minded determination to succeed has carried him to the top. He knows it has been a long path and that is why, even in the good times, he will never take anything for granted.

When Brian and I were players we loved every minute of our time at Aston Villa. I am delighted he is proving so successful at the club which means so much to both of us. He is bringing back the good times and long may they continue.

Andy Gray, July 1996

Chapter One

From East To West

It was in the pleasant surroundings of a hotel bar in Majorca that I discovered my predecessor, Ron Atkinson, had been dismissed as manager of Aston Villa.

Having spent a day in the sunshine, my wife Heather and I had gone downstairs for a drink before dinner and I decided to walk along to the shop for an English newspaper to catch up on the news back home. I have to admit, it was one of the last headlines I expected to read, but when I turned to the back page it screamed out at me that Ron had got the sack.

Heather and I had travelled over to Puerto Pollensa for a four-day holiday in November, 1994, at a time when there was a break in the Premiership programme. It was the first opportunity I had had to get away for a few days after undergoing a major back operation the previous summer.

Having spent five days in hospital, and then four or five weeks laid up at home, I had been unable to take any of Leicester's pre-season training in what was obviously going to be a big season for them back in the Premiership. Having to more or less organise from the side-lines, rather than being fully involved, was frustrating enough in itself. So I welcomed the chance of a short break away from it all.

So we were in Majorca for two reasons. Firstly, I had not been able to have a summer holiday because of back surgery. It had got to

November and I was only just about walking around properly, having had a section of vertebrae removed and my spine fused.

Some of you may recall it was a back problem which prevented my intended £600,000 move from Villa to Birmingham City when I was a player back in the 1978-79 season. I failed the medical and was told at the time to expect back trouble at some stage of my career. The specialist was right, although perhaps he didn't realise at the time that it would take 15 years for the problem to catch up with me.

The other reason for our visit to Majorca was that we always fancied buying a small apartment over there, so we had taken the opportunity to look round a few while we were away. It was a free two-week period for Leicester, and things had been a bit tough for me, so I found the trip an ideal way to get away and recharge the batteries.

It was something I had done several times in the past. I found it allowed me to clear my head and help make decent decisions, hopefully the right ones. So there we were, in Majorca, when I first found out that Villa no longer had a manager.

The fact that Ron had departed didn't influence me phoning my mother-in-law back home in Leicestershire that evening. But when I did phone her shortly afterwards, to see how our two sons Andrew and David were, she told me she had messages here, there and everywhere from Press guys wanting to speak to me, and that my name was already being linked with the Aston Villa vacancy.

I have to admit that during the five-minute walk back from the phone booth to the hotel I was already thinking about the Villa job. When it had become vacant three years earlier and, subsequently, went to Ron, I had actually got a mention then. But the word had come back to me, as it does in football, that I did not have enough experience at that particular time.

But now it was three years on. Having taken Leicester to three play-off finals, eventually into the Premiership, and the fact that all the Press were phoning my home, made me think that maybe I would be a serious contender for the vacancy.

I sat down with Heather that evening, told her that Ron had had the sack and the phone was going non-stop at home. In all fairness, one of her first questions to me was, would I do the job if I was asked. I have to admit that I immediately said 'yes, definitely!'

It was one of those situations where, deep down, I felt it was the right job, but possibly at the wrong time. However, those two ingredients very rarely come together, anyway.

My mother-in-law continued to take the calls but no one knew where I actually was, only that I had gone abroad. So during the last two days in Majorca no one was able to get in touch with me to talk about all the speculation back home. We returned to England on November 12, two days after Ron had left Villa, and that led to the chain of events which became so public and so well documented.

At no time did I ever give my full version of what was going on behind the scenes. I have kept quiet since then, despite being asked hundreds of times by everyone – from friends and family to football fans and the media – what really happened.

So here is my side of an incredible 13 days which ended with my appointment as Aston Villa manager on November 25, 1994 – which also happened to be my 41st birthday.

As soon as we arrived home that Saturday morning, November 12, I realised the enormous amount of interest I had created in my absence. When I turned on my car phone at Gatwick Airport there were, literally, scores of messages on the answer system. It seemed everyone from all sections of the media were keen to speak to me.

The messages were all of the same theme. They wanted my comments on the speculation that Aston Villa were interested in appointing me as their new manager. I realised I was among a number of candidates in the eyes of the media, who also included Graeme Souness, Steve Coppell, David Pleat and, my good friend, Bruce Rioch. As far as I was aware no public statement had been made by Aston Villa to support the speculation which surrounded me. The following day I continued to be contacted by members of the Press and asked to comment.

Questions were thrown at me suggesting that Mr Martin George, the chairman of Leicester City, had made certain comments, so I thought it was best to telephone him and arrange a meeting to discuss the situation before I talked publicly about it. We agreed to meet the following morning and it proved to be a very short meeting. I asked him what he had been saying to the Press and he reassured me he had made no public comment about all the speculation concerning me.

I told him I was pleased about that and just wanted to get on with my job at Filbert Street. Throughout the day the media continued to hound me, so I arranged another meeting with Mr George that afternoon at his office in Wellingborough.

It was during that meeting that he said he did not want to lose me as his manager and that he would say, if asked, that he had not given his consent to any approach from Aston Villa or any other club. We talked about a number of things concerning the speculation and I told him I was perfectly happy with my job at Leicester and we should issue a statement to that effect. I made it clear that the speculation was unsettling and I just wanted to resolve the matter and get on with my job. He told me his stance would not alter unless I informed him I wanted the opportunity to apply for the Villa job.

Although a Press statement was issued by Mr George outlining his determination to keep me a Filbert Street, for one of the few times in my life I felt very uneasy about a situation. I was happy that Mr George had made his feelings public but I still spent the whole of that evening chewing it over in my mind and didn't get too much sleep that night.

The following day, Wednesday, November 16, Mr George came to see me at Filbert Street in the middle of the afternoon. It was no surprise because he often used to put his head around the door for a chat. He didn't bring up the topic of Aston Villa – but I did!

I told him I had thought about the whole situation in much more detail, had discussed it with my wife, and said to Mr George I would like the opportunity to talk to Aston Villa if it presented itself. He simply replied he would consider what I had said, and walked out of my office. But I knew I had upset him.

It was only after my appointment as Villa manager that I learned that during this period of time Mr George had avoided telling me that contact had already been made between the two clubs, chairman to chairman.

I did not see or speak to Mr George during the following day but that evening we were together again for a social function at the football club. It was not really appropriate to discuss my request that I be given permission to talk to Villa, although I was disappointed that he had not come back to me in response to my request.

Our relationship that evening was strained and I think it was clear to everyone present, several hundred people, that all was not well between us.

The following day, November 18, I was concerned that I had not received any response from Mr George and I phoned him early that day. I said we needed to meet and try to sort things out. He replied that he was not available all day, so I arranged to travel to his home that evening in Stamford, Lincolnshire, to discuss the whole matter.

That meeting lasted at least an hour. It was, in the large part, amicable, and I took the opportunity to explain how much being the manager of Aston Villa would mean to me. Remember, I had joined Villa as a 15-year-old kid and it was the only club I ever wanted to play for.

I made my debut as a 17-year-old substitute against Blackburn Rovers in 1971. Six months later I completed my full debut in the Third Division 5-1 win over Torquay. Around 300 senior games later my playing days were ended by injury when I was 27.

After I had finished playing I worked for the club's Development Association for 12 months and then had a three-year spell as youth team coach. I also met Heather while I was at Villa. For 17 years the club had been my life and I only left to further my managerial career elsewhere.

I explained all this to Mr George during our meeting on November 18, in an attempt to show him the feelings I had for Aston Villa and the reasons why I wanted his permission, and his blessing, to apply for the vacancy. Mr George said he understood how I felt and, in turn, I informed him I was fully committed to remain in charge of Leicester City's first team for the Premiership match against Manchester City on the following Sunday.

I have to say at this point that during the course of our meeting I did indicate to him that if he refused me permission to speak to Aston Villa I would not want to continue as manager of Leicester City.

The meeting ended amicably, and he even gave me a brace of pheasant which he had shot that day. I think I spoke briefly to Mr George the following day about the game with Manchester City, but there was no further talk of our conversation from the previous evening.

The game against Manchester City on Sunday, November 20, was being screened live by Sky Television. There was continuing speculation about my position and Mr George was interviewed before the game kicked off. I watched the live interview from my office at Filbert Street.

At the time, I was under the impression that he and I had had a full and frank discussion, that he understood my desire to apply for the Villa job, and he was trying to resolve matters to enable me to do so.

Therefore, I was staggered by the comments he made during that television interview. It was as if our meeting the previous Friday had never taken place. He made it absolutely clear during the interview that I would not be given permission to talk to Aston Villa and that I would not be leaving Leicester.

I was very annoyed by his comments, not least because he had not taken the trouble to talk to me before speaking to the media. Knowing my position as he did, I had at least expected him to speak to me privately before making any further public statement.

We lost to Manchester City that afternoon, and I have to admit my mind was not entirely on the game because of what had been said publicly by my chairman before the match. I reported for work the following day, as normal, and went straight to see Mr George.

I told him how disappointed and angry I was about the comments he had made and that I was leaving Leicester. I told him that I would not work with him again under any circumstances, and left the keys of my BMW 730ISe club car on my desk. As far as I was concerned I had resigned there and then. Mr George said that he would like me to tell the Filbert Street board of my decision, which I agreed to do.

The following day – Tuesday, November 22, 1994 – will be etched in my memory for ever. I telephoned my secretary, Hayley, at Leicester, who also happened to be Mr George's secretary, because I knew a board meeting was taking place that morning. I asked her if she could arrange for me to meet the directors privately beforehand. Shortly afterwards she telephoned me to confirm they had agreed to my request.

As I drove from my home to Filbert Street I had alongside me a letter of resignation which I planned to hand in. No one can possibly imagine how many times I read that letter over and over in my mind. Once again I was about to put my career on the line.

Remember, I had walked out of my job as Aston Villa youth coach on a matter of principle when Graham Turner was in charge. I had been sacked at Wolves after only seven games as caretaker manager, and flatly refused any compensation, even though it was offered to me. I had resigned my post as reserve team coach at Middlesbrough Football Club even though I had the security of a two-year contract. I left because job satisfaction had deserted me. Never in my wildest dreams would I have gone behind manager Bruce Rioch's back at Ayresome Park and tried to find myself another job before handing in my resignation.

As I got nearer and nearer to Filbert Street I started reliving all those memories, all those principles that I had shown in the past. They were with me again, but I was still prepared to make the same sacrifices. Whatever the future held was irrelevant. I just knew I had to get away from Leicester City.

I arrived and met the board and read to them my letter of resignation. The board members were clearly concerned at the reasons I had given, in particular, the effect it might have on Mr George if it became publicly known that I had resigned because of the breakdown of my relationship with him.

They asked me in the strongest terms to withdraw my letter and to agree on a compromise announcement which would be in my best interests as well as his. They stressed that they did not want me to forget my own career prospects. As a result THEY suggested to ME that the statement I had made about not being the next Aston Villa manager should be withdrawn.

I was quite happy to look at a compromise announcement if one could be drawn up. I then left the meeting while they discussed the matter further. As far as I was concerned it had been agreed by the board that my original letter of resignation, in which I said I wanted to leave because of the breakdown in relationships with the chairman, was to be shredded, and no further reference was ever to be made to it.

A Press conference was called at Filbert Street later that day and the agreed statement was made public by the chairman. It read:

"The board of Leicester City Football Club wish to announce that Mr Brian Little has relinquished his position as team manager for personal reasons. These reasons have been discussed with the board, and his decision has been accepted with much regret. The board wishes to place on record their sincere thanks for the immense contribution made by Mr Little to the football club since he joined in the summer of 1991. Allan Evans will assume responsibility for the manager's duties at Leicester City until further notice."

Mr George was then specifically asked by members of the media if I was now free to join any club of my choice and his answer was strong and plain. Yes, I was!

A few hours earlier, when I left my home in the Leicestershire countryside, I had no idea what the future held. Now, all of a sudden, the opportunity was there for me to apply for the position of Aston Villa's manager, if I wished.

After the formal Press conference I was suddenly confronted by all sections of the media who all wanted one question answered: What was my next move, was I going to apply for the Villa job?

On reflection I should have said, yes. But I didn't because I was still coming to terms with the fact that Leicester had agreed to my release. Deep down it was the outcome I had hoped for but not expected, in view of all my previous experiences. I know I handled the Press badly that day, and I believe that goes a long way towards the ill-feeling there still is from certain sections of Leicester supporters. I had the opportunity to say publicly, there and then, that I wanted to become the next manager of Aston Villa. I had said it privately so many times but I missed my opportunity to make it known publicly, and that is something I have always regretted.

It was just a relief to get away from Filbert Street that day. For the first time in several days the opportunity was there for me to sit down, think clearly, and make my own decisions. I was no longer relying on the decisions of other people.

Once the dust had settled, one thing stuck out in my mind. I remembered being back in Majorca and being asked by my wife, Heather, the one person who means most to me, whether I would take the Villa job if the opportunity arose. My immediate reaction then was, yes, and on the strength of that I knew I had to speak to Villa chairman Doug Ellis.

I went home and weighed up all the options and later that night I contacted Mr Ellis and asked him if there was a chance of him talking to me about the position of Villa manager. He said there was, so I made an appointment to see him the next day, not at Villa Park but at his home.

I remember Mr Ellis suggesting it might be a bit more private at his house. As it turned out, when I arrived for the meeting there were several members of the local Press already waiting – probably not as many as there were at Villa Park but, nevertheless, I was photographed going into Mr Ellis's house and again when I came out several hours later.

I arrived for the meeting with Mr Ellis with only one thought in my head: I wanted to be the next manager of Aston Villa. I didn't go with any pre-conceived ideas about contracts or finances, or anything else like that. I simply made myself available for the vacancy.

As soon as the meeting began, the feedback that came from both the chairman and the club secretary, Steve Stride, was that they were very worried about the situation Villa were in. They had only won three League games up to then and at that particular time were only one point ahead of the club I had just left, Leicester City.

There wasn't much to choose between the two clubs at the time, but I was left in no doubt that there was serious concern at Villa Park that they were going to find it difficult to get out of trouble. So most of the talk that day was about how the chairman wanted to ensure that Villa would still be in the Premiership at the end of the season. I know the chairman would have given anything at that time in return for knowing that Villa would maintain their Premiership status.

We talked about the finances that might be available to keep the club up. He made it clear he was prepared to spend around £2m to £3m in the transfer market to try to ensure the club avoided relegation to the First Division.

That was a lot more than I had ever been given to spend before, so already there was a challenge for me. During the meeting I did make certain promises and put myself under pressure, because of the sort of person I am. I have to stress that I didn't ask for a penny for keeping Villa up. All I said to Mr Ellis was that I would want him to judge me as a manager at the end of the season and then, maybe, reward me with a better contract at some stage in the future.

I did not want to become Aston Villa manager for money, and if I failed I did not want to get money for not succeeding. It was of my doing, not his. I simply said to Mr Ellis that if I failed at his club he would not have to give me any money to sack me. There was no way I wanted money for the 'success' merely of keeping Villa in the Premiership.

When I joined Villa my personal financial package was very similar to the one I had at Leicester. If anything, I had more security at Leicester, based on the fact that I would pick up some compensation if I lost my job there. So once again I had stuck my head on the block, which looking at my previous track record was, perhaps, only what was to be expected.

It has been said since by certain parties in newspaper articles that by leaving Leicester and joining Villa I had jumped on the gravy train, which aggravates and annoys me, because I know for a fact that I did not. The job had become available, but I wanted to prove to people that I was doing it for the right reasons. So there was not much security in the contract for me.

I told Mr Ellis what I had been earning at Leicester and the Villa job was worth a little bit more. As I said, I sensed at that meeting that both the chairman and the secretary felt there was a problem at the club, so I feel that I took on the task of overcoming that problem for all the right reasons.

I suppose, looking back, I took on the job without a real contract, more a 'terms of agreement', with all the options on the club's side. But that was my doing more than anything else, so I'm not complaining. I just want to make it very clear that I did not walk out of Filbert Street and into Villa Park for financial security. That just wasn't the case.

When you go into a football club mid-season with the club not in the position everyone expects it to be, you always know you have got to make changes. But it is never easy to change things around at such a time. When I became manager at Leicester I went in during the close season where I had pre-season to work out what I wanted, and also do a bit of wheeling and dealing in the transfer market without too much trouble.

I suppose, in a way, taking the Villa job was similar to when I became manager at Darlington. I actually took that job in the February and failed to prevent them being relegated from the Football League into the GM Conference. I couldn't do much about the playing staff so late in the season, so I realised the problems that I might have in that same area at Villa.

I know we are talking about a Premiership club compared to one in the Third Division, but it was still a similar type of situation. Whatever League you are in you are still competing against teams at the same level when it comes to money being available to move into the transfer market.

All the clubs in a similar position to Villa that season were probably looking at the same players as myself, and had about the same amount of money to try to buy their way out of trouble. Maybe I was under a lot more pressure, because of the size and expectations of the club and the position they were in, but I didn't worry about that.

By the end of the meeting with the chairman and the secretary I knew in my own mind that I wanted to take on the challenge of keeping Villa in the Premiership. Mr Ellis and Steve Stride stressed that they knew their own jobs inside out, but they would not, for one minute, try to influence me about the playing staff and what was or was not required.

They told me there was a problem, that is why the job had become available in the first place, and it was up to me to sort it out. I have known the chairman for many, many years – ever since I joined Villa as a kid – and I could tell that he was very worried about Villa's prospects that season.

I also knew by talking to him just how big a decision it had been to let Ron Atkinson go because of the popularity of the man. I knew the chairman was under pressure because of that decision. While I had been popular as a player at Villa, in some people's eyes that counted for nothing when I was given the job as Ron's successor.

This was the biggest challenge I had ever faced in football. I knew from the media attention of the previous few weeks that I was going to be firmly in the spotlight. People were already questioning whether I was the right man for the job, and that was something I had never encountered before.

But that didn't stop me from wanting the job. I wanted to show the chairman, secretary and other people that I could do it. So I accepted the position with the sole aim of keeping Villa in the Premiership and then taking it from there.

The meeting at the chairman's house lasted four hours, but the patient Pressmen were still waiting. And when a press conference was called at Villa Park the following day I don't think there was much doubt that I was to become Villa's new manager. I was ready to make my move across the Midlands – from East to West.

After the meeting at the chairman's house I drove home, broke the news to Heather, and we went out for a meal to the Hilton Hotel at East Midlands Airport. We had a bottle of champagne because, I have to say, that this was always the job I had wanted but had never really admitted it to anyone. I remember telling Heather that night that I was about to experience the most difficult period of my football life and was taking on something that was very important to me. It could make or break my football career. This was something different, something very special. I told Heather to make the most of the meal because I envisaged that over the next few months we wouldn't be going out too much together.

By coincidence, the next day – the day of my official appointment – was my 41st birthday. But because of all that had been going on that fact had all but disappeared from my mind. It was only when I entered the Press conference and a few people started mentioning that it was my birthday, that it really sunk in.

Everything that day went well. Everyone now knew officially that I was the new manager of Aston Villa and I just hoped that it was going to be the end of what had been a very traumatic period in my life. There had been a lot of conflicting reports about my departure from Leicester and subsequent arrival at Villa but I was hoping this would be the end of it.

Maybe I should have known better...!

Chapter Two

Troubles Ahead

My first day in charge was fairly straightforward, and quite light-hearted. That was something of a blessing after all that had gone on in the previous ten days or so. I suppose, in a way, it was a relief to be formally introduced as the new manager.

It was one of those situations for me that I really wanted out of the way. It was handled well, and apart from the chairman and myself, John Gregory was also there to meet the Press lads. John had resigned from Leicester the same day as myself. When I left I sensed Mr George would ask Allan Evans, over and above John, to take charge of team affairs at Filbert Street.

I know John would not have liked that. Although Allan held the title of Assistant Manager and John was coach, they worked very evenly under me and, of course, still do. If Martin George had said to one of them that he wanted him to pick the team at the weekend then the other one would have walked out.

The way we work is a triangular sort of thing, with me at the top and Allan and John underneath in the corners, so to speak. Whichever one had been asked to stay on at Filbert Street, I know the other would have taken offence, so it didn't surprise me at all when John resigned.

He just wanted to get out of there, he didn't want to stay. Allan didn't especially want to stay either, but there was a lot of muck flying around so he agreed to stay for a few days, just to help them out. It's ironic that as a football manager he has had one game in charge in the Premiership, and beat Arsenal. That is one hell of a record!

But John came with me. I think he said what he had to say to Mr George and, in fairness, I don't think there was any real animosity between them. When you think about all the muck that flew around concerning myself, and then Allan later on, John got out of it without any problems at all. As you can imagine, 'Grego' is a bit of a lad who sometimes gets away with murder.

So John was there alongside me at the Press conference, and the day went well. We more or less just did what we had to and that was answer the usual barrage of questions from the newspaper boys, followed by loads of radio and television interviews.

When everyone had got what they wanted and disappeared, all I remember is walking along to the office which had 'The Manager' on its door, sitting down and realising I was manager of the place which, I have to say, was quite a weird feeling. I just let the whole thing wash over me for a while.

I sat back and recalled how I had been at this club as an apprentice, a young professional, and then a senior professional – even though I had had to pack up playing at a fairly young age – having worked in the club shop, and being a youth coach there. Now I was back as a 41-year-old and manager of the club.

As I was sitting there, I remembered my first ever day at Aston Villa. I thought, crikey, I can remember 1969 when I arrived here and the then chairman – a certain Doug Ellis – showed me, as he showed all the young apprentices, his Rolls Royce. I still remembered his words on that first day: "This is my Rolls Royce, and I am the chairman of this football club."

Now I was no longer that 15-year-old who had just left school, I was manager of the club, and that did mean a lot to me. It was a very proud moment. But it didn't take me long to realise that I didn't like my office one little bit. Things soon had to change.

When I looked around I thought this is no good to me. I knew I was going to work a lot from Villa Park. We have a magnificent training ground, but the way I work I believe it is important for me to be at Villa Park virtually every day. That is my choice, no one else's.

I spend a lot of time in my office, around the ground, thinking and planning, talking to people – be it the commercial department, the admin department, the secretarial department – because I like to know what's going on.

But I could tell that the manager's office at Villa Park was a place that had been used only now and again. I could see the training ground office was one that had been used on a regular basis, but that was not the case down at Villa Park.

I wanted and needed both to be spot on, not just one. When I have finished my work at the Bodymoor Heath training ground I invariably make my way to Villa Park. So I knew from day one that even when it came to offices there were things that I would have to do differently to my predecessor.

I also remember on my first day in charge that there was a rumour flying around – and at the time it was just a rumour – that Leicester were going to try to serve a court injunction to stop me from working, which really wasn't anything that I understood at that time. But, nevertheless, there was a rumour that it might well happen.

I suppose the most vivid memory for me was the day after my appointment when I took my first training session. That gave me a clear indication of what I had ahead of me because I have always been very much a training ground type of manager. In the previous three years John, Allan and I had got a group of players together at Leicester who, when they got to the training ground, knew what they were there for.

The minute they stepped out in their training kit they knew we were in charge. It was the same at Darlington when Frank Gray and I formed the managerial team. Once the training gear was on that was the signal for them to be ready and listening and do what was asked of them.

Maybe the Villa players were a little bit on their toes thinking there was a new fella coming in. But once the session started I just had to keep asking myself: "So is this really how top players react to training?"

I kept thinking to myself that I had been at Villa in 1981-82 when they won the League title, followed by the European Cup, and I could not recall the likes of Allan Evans, Peter Withe and Jimmy Rimmer not being properly prepared for training.

But here we were at my first training session, and all they had done was put on their kit and gone through the motions of doing a bit of work. Then I asked them to do what I refer to as 'acting' because I wanted to see a shadow-play training session.

Basically it entails putting eleven players out and letting them bring the ball down and pass it about with two-touch football, but without opposition, with each move finishing up with an effort on goal. So, in effect, the players were being asked to re-enact any situations which might occur on match days.

But what I saw was so disappointing it was untrue. When I was at Leicester and Darlington and picked a team of eleven players to do the same thing they were bright, lively and inventive. But here at Villa it seemed the players were all too busy taking the Mickey out of each other rather than concentrating on the training session.

I remember that morning thinking to myself that I had got an awful lot of work to do to make them operate the way I wanted to operate. It really sticks in my mind so vividly, it's untrue. Again, I wasn't as fit as I would liked to have been because I still hadn't recovered from my back problems.

But I was out on the training ground and wanted to put on a session that I had put on hundreds and hundreds of times in my previous five or six years as a manager, and had always had a lively, bright, enthusiastic response.

But there was a 100 per cent different response this time. It was as if it was a little bit beneath them. I knew they were good players, but even good players should respond to a training session. But I sensed they did not know how to play shadow-play, how to act and motivate each other without any opposition.

What struck me even more was seeing them a couple of hours later off the training ground where they were as lively, cocky and as mouthy as anyone I had ever come across in my life. And I think there and then it hit me just how much work I had to do.

I said to myself: "I haven't half got some troubles ahead." I have always maintained that it is on the field of play where you become the Jekyll and Hyde, not off it. You can be the nicest person in the world but when you get out on pitch that is when you change and really start showing what you can do.

But I just had a funny feeling that the group of players I had inherited were livelier, noisier and showed off more when they were off the field of play rather than on it. Yes, you can win matches with that approach, but let's not forget they had only won three all season.

Maybe energies were being channelled in the wrong directions. For me, the place to show off is on the field of play. When I was a footballer I always regarded myself as a fairly quiet fella. But I know I showed off when I had a football at my feet. But here we were with players who were showing off in the wrong places at the wrong times.

That is how I felt from day one. Yes, they were good players, but they were not right as far as I was concerned. I was disappointed, and when I looked closely at the situation I suppose I wasn't surprised at the lowly League position they were in because, in all fairness, you could see there was talent there, but something was wrong. The atmosphere wasn't right and there were attitude problems.

I don't care what sport you are in, I maintain you cannot turn up on your sporting day and put it into practice if you don't practice through the week. The best golfers in the world spend hours on the practice ground before they go out to play in a tournament. Athletes, tennis players, snooker players –you can go on and on – they practice to find perfection.

I don't think the training ground is a place just to have fun. Sure, you have a bit of fun but at the same time you have to work hard and practice. There has to be a method as to what you are doing. I am a great believer that the training ground is a place of work, and when you get there you are there for someone to teach you.

On that first day I saw my role and that of John Gregory as being teachers, but I was given the impression that no one wanted us to teach, and that disappointed me.

The next thing I had to look at during those initial days was the coaching staff. During my days as youth team coach, reserve team coach, or even first team coach at my previous clubs, I always felt it was important to be 100 per cent in vogue with the manager. So it was important to me that the people I had inherited were going to be the same as myself in that respect. When I arrived I think there were a few worried faces around, from kitman Jim Paul to physio Jim Walker, fitness coach Paul Barron, youth team coach Colin Clarke and chief scout Brian Whitehouse. All I did early on with these guys was to sit down and tell them that within a month or two we would know whether we could work with each other.

When I was a coach I was never frightened to tell people to their faces, "Don't do this and don't do that," rather than talk about people behind their backs. And as a coach I always approached the manager to talk to him, not wait for him to come running after me.

So now I was a manager and the minute I walked out of a room I didn't want people to say behind my back, "I'm glad he has gone."

At the same time, if I had to go off somewhere I wanted to know I had left matters in safe hands, with people adopting the same principles and believing the way I believed. It is a very important aspect of management, having the full belief that the people who are around you are also 100 per cent behind you.

As a manager I didn't expect to have to go around chasing people. I expected them to come to me, ask me if there was anything I needed doing, or did I require any of the youth team to put anything out for training sessions.

Ultimately you have to make decisions, often unpopular, when you feel you cannot get on with certain people, or that they are not doing their job as you want them to. And there was a lot of controversy in the case of Colin Clarke who, up until the day I decided we should part company, had actually won 18 straight games with his youth team.

Yet there was so little conversation between Colin and myself it was untrue, and in defence of myself I didn't think that I should have to go running around after him as was often the case. As a youth coach I made sure my manager had anything he wanted before I went about my business. But although Colin was doing his own job well there was no communication between us.

I have to have people around me who are comfortable in my presence, and vice versa. But there always seemed a discomfort between us when we were together.

The fact that he had had a fair amount of success with the team that season meant I got quite a bit of flak when he was sacked, not least of all from Colin, because it came as a major disappointment to him. He told me straight to my face, in no uncertain terms, that he wasn't happy with my decision.

But he had a one year contract at the club and was looked after financially by the chairman. In fairness, a relationship between Colin and I would never have taken shape because of the way I run a club.

Don't get me wrong, those are the sort of decisions that, as a manager, you hate making. Some people may think that when managers sack people they are doing it just to be ruthless. But that is not the case. I was just trying to provide for the chairman and supporters at Aston Villa, and for me to do that everything had to be right around me.

Now we can look 18 months or so down the road and see that the team Tony McAndrew inherited from Colin won the Midland Purity Youth League. And in his second season with a new team Tony won the same League again. So the decision to make a change has been justified in many respects.

The second person to leave was Brian Whitehouse who, I have to say, is a lovely man. His departure came about following what can only be described as an unsettling rumour which appeared in a local sports paper.

It suggested that Malcolm Beard, who worked for me part-time at Leicester as chief scout, was coming to Villa to rejoin me. I must say that although Malcolm left Filbert Street at the same time as I did, I never spoke to him at that particular time about coming to Villa.

Brian saw the newspaper article, came in to see me, and said that if that was what I wanted then he would rather leave and do something different. It was all very amicable between us. He knew by then that Ron Atkinson had got himself fixed up at Coventry, and he and Ron had always worked closely together at Manchester United as well as Villa.

But he was concerned about the rumour which had appeared and on the strength of that, more or less offered his resignation. I am sure Brian is happier back working with Ron. But it just shows you how dangerous gossip and speculation in newspapers can be, because it can cause problems like the one I had to encounter with Brian.

If I had £1 for every time a player had knocked on my door and said: "What about that story about me in the paper today?" then I would be a wealthy fella. But I suppose that is an aspect of the game that keeps my job interesting.

So with Colin and Brian I had two contrasting departures. Colin very unhappy with me but Brian very much at ease. I have to emphasise both were difficult decisions, but ones which were made to try get things right at the club.

As I mentioned earlier, when John Gregory and I left Leicester Allan Evans was left in limbo, staying in charge for one game. But Allan knew that whoever the new manager was to be at Filbert Street, he would become surplus to requirement. So he was prepared to do the one game and then move on. That was always going to happen.

So the fact that Leicester would not accept his resignation made it very awkward for Allan. That meant him having to spend several weeks at home not being involved in the game, and having to content himself by doing the washing, ironing and gardening. But in fairness to Allan he is probably the world's best dad-cum-husband. We rib each other something rotten about it, because although I am all right when it come to a bit of gardening, I don't know one end of an iron from the other!

I am sure many will remember Allan as that big, hard, central defender who helped Villa win the League Championship and European Cup back in the early 1980's. But he is such a smashing fella and so domesticated off the field. Even so, I think five or six weeks at home doing the chores even tested him to the limit.

There were also many times during that spell when John and I looked at each other and said: "We wish Evo was here." All three of us are very different as individuals but there are areas in which we specialise, and one corner of the triangle was missing.

We work like clockwork together and John and I were missing

Allan being around. It was difficult trying to tie it all in together without Allan, who helps me with training and also off the field of play, making sure players are here, there and everywhere, attending functions or making presentations.

He also helps me with my work down at Villa Park, organising my scouting trips and the like, so there was a big sigh of relief from John and myself when Allan finally rejoined us.

We had gone through an awkward couple of months trying to make things tick, without him being there to play his part.

It was during the time that Allan wasn't around that we played our first match with me as the manager. It was against Sheffield Wednesday, managed at that time by Trevor Francis, someone who has always been a good friend. We grew up in Birmingham together in terms of our playing careers, albeit in opposite camps, myself at Villa Park and Trevor at St Andrew's.

Quite often in our younger days comparisons were drawn between the two of us. Trevor later went on to establish himself as a Premiership manager, taking Wednesday to both the FA Cup and League Cup Finals. Now he is back at St Andrew's and I would like to wish him all the best for the future with Birmingham City. He will be trying to establish himself back at St Andrew's just as I was during my first game back at Villa.

I received a tremendous reception from the Villa supporters that day, but I sensed that although people wanted me to do well there was still that doubt area of whether I could do well – whether I was the right man for the job. Was I the person with enough experience and know-how to save this big club from dropping out of the Premiership, at a time when it was becoming more and more important to be up there among the elite?

In fairness to Ron he had had a terrific spell, but then a few months when things had gone wrong. It was one of those spells that can happen to any football manager. You know only too clearly if you get into a run of 15 or 20 games of not doing so well, then the modern pressures of the game tend to make things like his departure happen.

I have always had a healthy respect for Ron and when I went into the job at Villa I knew it would be a difficult act to follow, based on the fact that I am so different to him. I am the sort of person who has to work to precision. I have to sit down and put a lot of thought into my preparation for a game. I want things to be spot-on leading up to it.

On the other hand, Ron is the sort who can just walk in and make things happen at any particular time. I am not saying Ron is not organised – he is probably a very organised guy – but he is also very much a presence guy, whereas I don't rely on presence. I rely 100 per cent on organisation and preparation.

If I go into a game and I am not happy it is very difficult for me to make it right on the day. I have to have everything leading up to it right and proper. So I suppose that is what makes us two totally different types of manager.

When I walked out at Villa Park in front of more than 25,000 that day in November, 1994, for my first game in charge, I don't think too many people expected me to be jumping about, waving my arms in the air, and making everybody think: "Wow, this guy is really going to be it." I have always found that side of management difficult.

In my playing days, just give me a football and let me go out and I would show off, but as a manager I can never see myself jumping up and down and shouting about.

During a game I am as intense as anyone but I like to let my feelings known to my players in the dressing room at half time, and sometimes even after a match, although not so much immediately afterwards, because people's feelings and emotions tend to be running high when you have just walked off the pitch. If you say too much it can lead to problems. There are times when I am as volatile as anyone, in my own way. But I genuinely sensed on that first day supporters were saying it was good to have me back. But they were wondering if...

The game itself went great for 45 minutes. I thought the lads played ever so well, credit to them, and Dalian Atkinson put us in front. But we were very nervy in the second half. We were 1-0 up, but clubs under pressure often tend to lose such advantages and, as we ran out of steam a bit, Peter Atherton got Wednesday's equaliser.

My team was solid enough but I already knew we didn't have the

31

mobility, or the ability, to get at the opposition for 90 minutes. There were things niggling at me and one thing that worried me was how much surgery I would be able to do mid-season.

I had always done a lot of transfer work during the close season at my previous football clubs. In my first summer as the Darlington manager I moved out 20 players in one day. Within seven months of being in charge at Leicester I had been involved in 30 transfer dealings, the majority of them in the summer.

Now I was thinking how much I could do, how long would it take me to change things around, how would the players I had inherited respond to me now we had played our first game together? These players were household names, with stronger characters, in many respects, than I had dealt with before.

So I knew there was work to be done. But how difficult it was going to be was something that was giving me genuine cause for concern.

Chapter Three

Court Victory, Cup Defeat

Although I do not intend to detail every match that season, I have to say that the next two games, and the circumstances surrounding them, were among the most traumatic of my entire managerial career.

Three days after we had drawn with Sheffield Wednesday, we had to prepare ourselves for a trip to Crystal Palace in the fourth round of the Coca-Cola Cup. Although Ron had gone, he had guided Villa to success in this competition the previous March. So after victories over Wigan and Middlesbrough before I arrived, we were going to Selhurst Park looking for a place in the quarter-finals.

Excuses come thick and fast in football, but if ever there was a night when excuses could be justified then that game was probably the one.

Our first setback came when Kevin Richardson had a back spasm an hour or two before the game, which ruled him out. Then Ugo Ehiogu got sent off fairly early in the game, and Dalian Atkinson came off with a hamstring strain shortly after he had put us ahead. We never saw Dalian back in action for ages after that.

I remember we ended up playing Dwight Yorke at right-back in the second half. If I can transport my mind forward 18 months or so, the thought of playing Dwight at full-back now would horrify me. But at the time he was playing regularly on the right side of midfield as opposed to an out-and-out striker, so moving him back just one place to full-back didn't seem that unusual to me.

It was just one of those nights when so many things went against us. It is history that we lost the match 4-1 and relinquished our hold on the Coca-Cola Cup. There were a lot of things which disappointed me.

After the game I had my first real opportunity to talk to the players for a good 10 to 15 minutes and I spelled it out, in no uncertain terms, that things would have to be done my way. They would have to comply with my thinking, with my rules.

I learned a lot that night. I saw things that my players could and could not do. So this was the opportunity for me to say: "Right, fellas, I've been with you for a week and it is time you realised I am the boss."

Overshadowing everything, though, was the fact that Leicester City had decided to take me to High Court to seek an injunction preventing me from continuing my work as Villa manager. The hearing in London was on the very day that we played Palace in the Coca-Cola Cup. The rumours flying around before the Sheffield Wednesday game proved right.

I had already made a sworn statement about my side of events which led to my departure from Filbert Street. So although I didn't attend court my statement was to be read out that day.

I was down in the team hotel in London, patiently awaiting the outcome. At the same time I was trying to prepare my team for a very important game. The hearing seemed to drag on for ever. Whenever I rang to see if it was over I was told, either it had not even started, or it was still continuing.

In fact, I did not know the outcome of the hearing until after the match that night, so I suppose you could call it "won one, lost one." Although I was told afterwards that I had won that side of it, the legal business still wasn't all over because Leicester had an opportunity to appeal within 30 days.

As I explained earlier, I knew my resignation at Leicester had been accepted, so why was I going through this? Why was I being taken to court when several days earlier a statement had been read out at

Filbert Street to the effect that I could leave? Mr George had publicly stated that I was free to take on any other job, including the one at Aston Villa.

So it was all very confusing for me and a situation which I did not enjoy one bit. I am not one of those guys who would call himself a goody-goody, but I did not think I had done anything wrong. The fact I had been taken to court was quite a trouble to me. It was something that perhaps made me quieter than I should have been going into a new club.

When you take on a new job you want to be bright and bubbly and to impress on people how much in control you can be. Yet I wasn't really what I should have been because of all this other stuff going on around me, which was concerning me, to say the least. Still, unless there was to be an appeal from my former club, I had won the court case. That allowed me to prepare for the next game – the infamous return to Filbert Street to take on Leicester City.

The problems began as early as eight o'clock on that Saturday morning when I was about to leave my home and drive over to meet up with the players in an hotel for the pre-match meal and preparations. I received a phone call from a good friend suggesting I ought to read the back page of one of the national newspapers.

So I stopped off at the newsagent to buy one and then I saw the headline "Little Liar" shouting out at me. It shook me a bit, to be perfectly honest. A lot of people that day would have probably read the headline and dismissed it. But when it concerns you and it is your name that is up there, then it can be quite hurtful.

The story included an extract from my original letter of resignation given to Leicester, which the directors had asked me to withdraw and, I believed, had been shredded. To this day I don't know how it got out and why it had not been destroyed, as had been promised.

I know in my own mind there are up to three places it could have come from, three people who could have leaked it to the Press. It could have been any one of the three or any combination of the three. But that doesn't bother me any more.

I don't really want to know who it was, who was prepared to go behind my back and reveal something which I had been asked to withdraw, and did so at the request of the Filbert Street board.

But one thing is for sure, it certainly stirred up the Leicester supporters that day for our match over there. The headline could have come almost at any other time of my life and would not have had anywhere near the same impact.

I can still see to this day so many Leicester fans holding up pieces of paper, with just one word written on it: LIAR!

The reception I received at the game was arguably as hot and hostile as anyone has ever had to endure in football. Leicester supporters are lively, to say the least. I had some great rapport with them for three and a bit years. Between us we drummed up so much support and enthusiasm to win games for Leicester.

I knew that day, when they were going to be angry at me, crikey, they were really going to be angry – and they didn't let me down in that respect! A lot of people said I should not have been surprised at the reception I received. But I have to say the ferocity of it did just that.

That one headline, that one story, influenced every Leicester fan 100 per cent. I can't imagine that even one Leicester supporter who saw that headline just put down the paper and dismissed it. They all believed it, so it had an unbelievable effect on people who genuinely had a lot of time for me only weeks earlier.

I maintain that what had been done was underhand. But one of the things which really disappointed me was the fact that no one had put two and two together and come up with four. They all got the sum wrong, because it was all weighted too heavily against me.

One thing you find in relationships between football managers and the Press is that you rarely get the chance to respond before the original story appears – because it takes the edge off it. So you never get that opportunity to reply and, in many cases, put the record straight. I have come to learn and understand that. I accept, to a point, that a story does not have as much impact if it has an answer to it. By the time you get the chance to answer, more often than not, it doesn't really matter because that first opinion is invariably the one that people stick with.

So I was given a real noisy 'welcome' that day, with shouts of

"Judas" also being levelled at me. There was so much feeling and passion from Leicester fans it was almost physical. But people pay their money to go inside a football stadium and have a good shout, so they were entitled to say what they wanted. Thankfully, it never sprang up outside the stadium, which was important to me.

As far as the game was concerned, I remember Leicester taking the lead when Nigel Spink made a mistake, allowing Phil Gee to score after only five minutes. But we managed to get back into it and a goal from Guy Whittingham earned us a draw. At the end of that game Villa were still only a point ahead of Leicester in the battle to stay up.

I still get a bit of stick every now and again, but time heals. If the problems involving the Leicester fans had become any worse then I would have had to consider moving from our home in Leicestershire, which was something the family and I did not want to do. We were very happy there – and still are – and didn't want to be forced to leave. I didn't want to run away from anything or anybody.

So in the space of a few days I had endured the completely new experience of being taken to court, followed by defeat in the Coca-Cola Cup, and then going back to Filbert Street for my red-hot reception. I hope Leicester do well in future, but I left because I felt I had taken them as far as I could and it was time for someone else to take over.

There is no animosity, as far as I am concerned, about what happened that day. I had three good years at the club and the experiences there have, hopefully, helped me become a better manager. I have a lot to thank the club for, in many respects.

The day was as it was because of an article in a newspaper. But all I wanted to do after that was go home and shut the door behind me.

Chapter Four

No Mugs, Please!

Since I became Villa manager, and even in my previous jobs after I finished playing, I know I have often been criticised for looking too serious, even miserable, and not letting any emotions show through. There has been mockery from certain quarters, even from my two kids. When I get home after being on television they will always ask: "Why didn't you smile, dad?"

Yes, I am more serious now than I used to be. It is all down to the fact that I had the experience of enjoying myself as a player and then one day waking up, having hurt myself, and realising that I was never going to play again.

I wasn't a bad professional but I just took things very easy and very much for granted, perhaps believing it would go on a lot longer than it did.

I think I was a good team player. I don't think the likes of Andy Gray, John Deehan and Keith Leonard, who I played alongside, would say I was selfish on the field of play. But I have seen quotes from Andy saying he didn't think I would ever be a good manager because of my attitude as a player.

That is fair enough, I used to do my own thing, and still do now. As an individual I am very strong minded and I learned from the experience of having my playing career taken away from me when I was still only 27.

So now when you see me as a manager, standing on the touchline, I am working, taking it all in, trying to make sure I don't miss anything. Then if it did all come to an end tomorrow, just as it did as a player, I could turn round and say that I gave it everything I had got.

Don't get me wrong. I am not 100 per cent serious all the time – but I am about my work, and what people say about me doesn't worry me. I have a strong desire to do the things I think are right. If other people tell me to do things and I feel they are right, then I will do them – but I will never do anything for anybody that I don't agree with. That would be against all my principles. I could never see myself doing something just for the sake of it. I would rather turn round and say that I couldn't do it, so ask someone else.

I won't say I am always right, but at least people, like my players, know where they stand with me. I don't have to bawl and shout at them. If I don't get what I want then they know what to expect. As a football manager you buy players and mould them to do what you believe is right and proper. If they do not fall into that category with me then they tend to move on.

I don't fall out with those guys, I simply tell them that they are not doing what I want, they don't play the way I want them to play, so I am going to help them get a career somewhere else. I think my mentality has come through in that way in the dressing room. I don't really have bust-ups with players, or belittle anyone in front of colleagues. I don't like that, I didn't like it if I was ever picked on as a player and singled out for criticism.

I do not believe any player goes out on the field to deliberately make a mistake. Everyone wants to do well. So, with that in mind, I try to level criticism on a constructive basis rather than a destructive one. I do not do something because I have seen someone else do it. I do it because I believe in it. I have always been my own man, doing what I want to do, going where I want to go. That's just me.

I wouldn't call myself dour. I just like to concentrate on the job in hand, and make sure I know what is going on around me. That overtakes everything on a match day. I see some people in the game, almost entertaining to a point, killing a bit of time by having a chat to folk before a match. I can't do that.

When I wake up on the morning of a game, at home rather than away in a team hotel, even my wife and kids leave me alone, because they know I am thinking about what I have got to do that particular day. And when anyone tries to break that routine they become a hindrance to me and I let them know it, to the point of having upset a lot of people over the years.

Before and after a match people sometimes see a side of me they perhaps didn't know existed. I am liable to snap at them if they get in my way. I am often asked to do television interviews before a game but I find that an intrusion into the more important things I am trying to do. I know I may have to talk to people after matches and that is a bit easier, giving television interviews and talking to the Press.

But before a match, I invariably ask Allan Evans to go and stand in front of the cameras because I am focused on what I am doing and don't want to go off the path. It's not superstition or anything like that, it is just that I am trying to do my job to the best of my ability.

But when I get back home there is a totally different me. I am able to switch off, very much so. I love to sit and relax and watch a lot of television. I might be reluctant to give television interviews before games but when it comes to watching then it's fair to say I am very much a television man.

I also enjoy playing and having a laugh and joke with my kids, Andrew and David, who are 14 and 11 years old, the right age to enjoy having around you. Heather and I also like to sit down late in the evening and have a meal together, a chat and maybe a glass of wine.

Even when it comes to eating I like things to be right. When I was at home as a kid I had to sit down at a table and eat, rather than be in front of a television with the plate on my knee. Food has to look nice on the plate. I have always been a bit of a perfectionist in that respect.

Even when I am at work you will never find me drinking tea out of a mug. It has to be in a cup with a saucer. If I go anywhere and people ask me if I want a cup of tea or coffee and then bring it out in a mug, I just can't drink it.

It can be quite embarrassing at times. If ever I am out with Allan and John, they often joke: "Make sure you give him a cup and saucer, or he won't drink it."

I like the right presentation. If I have people around to my home I pride myself in looking after them properly. I am that sort of creature but, at the same time, there are other things about me you may find surprising.

For example, we have been in our present home a few years now. But not so long ago the gas man called to read the meter while Heather was out. I told him he would have to come back because I had no idea where the meter was.

Because I am out so much, the running of the home, the paying of the bills, the setting up of everything to do with home life is down to Heather. Basically, I haven't got a clue how our home functions. I can cook a bit, but not very often. But I wouldn't know the first thing about paying the telephone bill or renewing the television licence.

So I suppose you could call it a reversal of roles and different in many ways to, perhaps, some of the guys who come down to Villa Park to watch us play. I enjoy gardening because I find that an excellent way to relax away from work. I wouldn't say I was particularly green-fingered, but I like to see nice lawns and tidiness.

I spend hour after hour around the outside of my home, and my youngest lad loves to help, whereas the older one is very much into computers and music and tends to shut himself away more to do his own thing. I have always been capable of looking after myself and I can see Andrew very much down that same line.

David, however, is the one who needs the attention and loves to be out in the garden working with me. As well as a big garden we also have a stable block with about five acres of land. David likes nothing more than to be out there with me on tractor mowers, cutting the grass. I have recently bought a third tractor mower, hoping to persuade Andrew to join in. But I think I might be on to a loser there.

I have often thought it might be nice to have animals of some sort on my land, whether it's horses, sheep or cattle. But we haven't quite got round to that yet. However, we do keep eight chickens in one of the areas in the field, trying to ensure that the foxes stay well away.

So we get our fresh eggs every day and I have often toyed with the idea of trying to become self-sufficient – 'The Good Life', so to speak. But if I took that on just now I think I would be taking on a bit too much. However, my home life lends itself to getting away from my work load.

I am in a high profile job and, whether I like it or not, I am recognised when I walk down the street. So my home life allows me to leave that a million miles away. We do have neighbours but we are still very private.

For example, we had been in the house about a year and I was down at the bottom of my land when I saw this person I didn't know walking across it. I was about to tell him that he couldn't walk through there, because it was private, when he introduced himself – as my next door neighbour!

Now I wouldn't call myself a bad neighbour, it's just that when I do get home from a day's work I can switch it all off. I know some people enjoy the buzz and excitement of being among folk 24 hours a day, but I don't. I wouldn't say I was a recluse, but I like to avoid crowds, and the hustle and bustle when I am away from my work. I much prefer being around my home, if not watching television, then out working in the garden.

Music also plays an important part in my life, especially when I am driving the many miles I cover each year, either to and from work, or travelling around the country watching football matches. I suppose I am something of an individual when it comes to music. Many people will look at me and think that because I am in my 40's I'm into Frank Sinatra and the likes.

Well, although I enjoy music like that to a degree, I am far more into the new music wave – the likes of Oasis, Counting Crows and Horse. The last two many of you may not have heard of. I suppose it's more for the younger element. But I like listening to their music.

I am also still into groups like Pink Floyd, Black Sabbath and Deep Purple, a throwback to my younger days. Then there is the American stuff like James Taylor and Carly Simon, so I have a real diverse taste in music.

Sometimes, if I give one of my players a lift in my car, or have just completed a transfer deal and am taking the new man to Villa Park or the training ground, they can hardly believe their ears when I switch on the CD player in my car. I can see them giving me a funny sideways look and thinking: What sort of music is this? What sort of fella is this I'm with?

So although inside me there is Brian Little the football manager, there is also Brian Little the individual, who does what he wants to do and sometimes loves to get away from it all. Whatever happens to me in life, I believe I will always maintain those strong feelings for being very much an individual, very much my own man.

Chapter Five

Wheeling and Dealing

The transfer market has always been a bit of a pet of mine, even when I was at Darlington and I was given £40,000 to spend, then in my first season at Leicester when I was told I could spend £250,000. You know you have to spend it wisely.

When I got the Villa job, I had a conversation with the chairman who suggested I had around £2.5m to try to get the team out of difficulty, maybe a little bit more if really necessary, but after that I knew I had to wheel and deal in the market.

I knew all about that because at Darlington I bought just one player with the £40,000, a lad called Andy Toman, from local rivals Hartlepool. Then I had to wheel and deal for the rest.

But you always know that when you start moving into the transfer market it can be a bit of a minefield. So many times you read of players who have been bought by clubs and then can't settle. There is rarely a doubt about players' ability but sometimes off-the-field problems, like settling into a different area, can make them look almost bad players when, in fact, they are not. So spending money can be a delicate operation, and something that can make or break you as a manager in many respects.

I find one of the worst parts of the whole job is when it comes to giving a young lad a free transfer. Since I have been at Villa I have released ten young lads. There is some consolation in the fact that if a lad of 19 or 20 has had a few years at a club like Villa, then maybe he has enough of a background to get an opportunity somewhere else. But it is still a difficult task, probably the least enjoyable of the job.

Can you imagine sitting there with a young lad and telling him face to face: "I'm sorry we don't think you are good enough and in three or four weeks time your wages will be stopping." Of the ten, I actually signed two of them as full time professionals and then released them, so that makes it even worse.

It's a horrible experience. But one of the things I always tell them is that if they go on and make a good career in the game for themselves, don't think I will be embarrassed by it. I always tell them that I hope I am wrong in letting them go.

That is proving to be the case as far as a young lad called Dennis Pearce is concerned. We released him in the summer of 1995 and since then he has forced his way into the first team at Wolves. Now maybe people will think I should try to hide that fact, or even ignore it altogether, but far from it. Actually, I am pleased for Dennis.

He wasn't getting an opportunity at Villa. He had been at the club four years and couldn't even get into the reserves on a regular basis. In the pecking order for the left-back spot he was behind the likes of Steve Staunton, Phil King, Bryan Small and later Alan Wright, so his chances of playing were next to none.

So while it can be a big 'downer' for kids who are released, if they have enough spirit about them and have had a few years at a club like this, hopefully, it gives them the grounding to find something else. Having said that, I still maintain it is one of the worst parts of my job, telling youngsters there is no longer room for them.

Then I have to deal with free transfers from within the established professional ranks, with Nigel Spink the ideal example. What a fabulous servant Nigel was to Villa for more than 18 years. So to help him get a good two-year deal at West Bromwich Albion, a club where he didn't have to uproot his family and move house, I was happy to release him knowing it would be of benefit to him.

Nigel was nothing but 100 per cent supportive of me from the day I walked into this job. So I would like to think that by letting him go it was as a 'thank you' for everything he had done to help me.

Bryan Small also left on a 'free.' I have known Bryan since he was 12-years-old and I was youth team coach at Villa. He was a lad who came up through the ranks but found that other players were invariably bought ahead of him, and he became nothing more than a stand-in.

So, perhaps, even before I arrived, his career was going backwards at Villa. He was picked occasionally for specialist jobs because of his pace and defensive ability. But he was never going to be regarded as number one choice. He was available for a long time without anyone taking him. In the end he was given the chance to leave on a free transfer and that interested several clubs before he decided to join Bolton. So I am pleased for Bryan and hope he goes on to have a successful career in the game.

During my first 18 months at Villa I was able to look back and realise that I had dealt with around 50 players when it came to transfers in, transfers out, and negotiating new contracts, which also falls into this category. There were ten major signings during that time, with ten youngsters also signing pro contracts. Then there were 24 players who moved on and another 14, or so, who have been involved in new contract talks. So, as you can imagine, the transfer side of things takes up a lot of time.

The days of sitting down with a player and half an hour later having a signed a contract are long gone. When I was a player there were no agents and financial advisers. I remember walking in to negotiate my own deal, thinking that if the manager didn't meet my demands I would give him some right stick.

Then before I knew it, I would be coming out of his office, nowhere near as well off as I hoped I would be, after being given the ultimatum: Sign that, or you are out!

It was intimidating for players a few years ago. It was easy to look into the mirror and rehearse what you were going to say to the manager. But when it came to the crunch it was an entirely different matter. The manager would always be the winner.

Nowadays, players have agents, advisers, call them what you want, and that gives them a strength which makes it difficult for the manager, the chairman, or other people who oversee the finances of a club.

On top of that we are about to go into an era when the name Bosman comes very much into the equation. No one is absolutely sure what is going to happen, although we all believe that at some stage we shall be talking about players who are out of contract being free agents, whatever.

It will bring a massive change to the game as we know it, if that is the case. Supporters will have to come to terms with the fact that players will be free to move here, there and everywhere. I think the modern trend will be for players to sign two-year contracts, maximum, so they can move on and play where they want, provided they are good enough.

For them to be that choosy is a completely different slant on how football has been in the past. It is all right for a kid to say he wants to play for Villa, Manchester United, or whoever. But, until now, that club had to be prepared to buy you, probably for big money.

It seems that in the very near future players who are good enough will be able to choose where they go. So that, to my mind, is about to change the whole face of the game as we know it. Considering all the transfer deals I have been involved in over the past seven years, or so, it will be quite a phenomenal change that is about to take place.

But if I now go back to the transfer deals, in and out, since I arrived at Villa, then I suppose it is fair to say there has been a certain amount of controversy in many respects. Some very well established players have left the club. You can look back on names such as Dalian Atkinson, Earl Barrett, Ray Houghton, Garry Parker, Kevin Richardson, Dean Saunders, Shaun Teale, Nigel Spink, and for a different reason, John Fashanu.

They had provided the nucleus of the team for a couple of seasons before I arrived, so to move out so many of them in such a short time was quite a brave step, although I have to say that at one stage I realised that by letting so many go put us under threat far more than needed to be.

It became obvious to me that I had to make changes, probably a lot more than even the chairman imagined. I think he expected me to make some, but the fact I made so many made a lot of people sit up, not just the chairman.

If the opportunity comes along to be involved in a transfer deal and I know, deep down, it is the right thing to do for the long term then, more often than not, I go for it. But in some respects I almost paid the price for that.

The sale of some of the more experienced players came at a time when we had recovered in the Premiership to the point of climbing towards mid-table, and even beyond. Indeed, there was some talk that we might qualify for a place in Europe the following season. But by selling Kevin Richardson, Ray Houghton and, to a degree, Garry Parker, I lost some of the competition for midfield places.

Suddenly the competitive edge and balance had gone, which I knew I was not going to be able to replace until the close season. I genuinely felt at one stage that we had moved away from the relegation area and were safe. I am sure most of our supporters felt the same way. However, as we all know, those last eight or ten games, which I shall go into more detail later, became a bit of a nightmare for me, based on the brave decision to let these guys go.

In fairness, however, the offers had been received for players like Richardson, Houghton and Parker, who were finding themselves on the substitutes' bench for possibly the first time in their Villa careers. Their presence still provided the competitive edge for first team places, but I made it clear to them that if offers came in we would sit down and talk about them.

Offers did come in for all three players, and they had the opportunity to say they did not want to leave us. But they all knew they were at the stages of their careers where playing first team football was the most important thing. So after they had had discussions with their respective new clubs it wasn't really difficult for them to decide to move on.

Of the three, I think Kevin was perhaps the most disappointed. I think he genuinely wanted to play at Villa. He was club captain when I arrived at Villa Park and only a few months earlier had proudly lifted the Coca-Cola Cup at Wembley before going on to win an England cap. But deep down he knew that if he wasn't going to be a regular in the first team he had to consider his future and, in the end, decided it was the best thing for him to move to Coventry.

Before he went he voiced his disappointment, which was understandable. But, as I have said, he had the option to stay if he wanted. So I have no feelings of guilt that I forced him out of the place. At the end of the day it was his decision to leave. I knew he, Gary and Ray were good players, but they were not regularly in the side and they were at the wrong age not to be first team players.

I have always emphasised that I have never had a hang-up about picking a team. I always select the side I feel is right for that particular day. I never sit in my office thinking that if I leave a certain player out he will be knocking on my door on Monday morning, demanding to know why, and having a right moan at me. It doesn't worry me that if I pick a team without someone and we lose, then invariably the Press are going to give me a hard time.

I genuinely dismiss all those feelings from my mind and select the team I believe to be right. Then, if there are problems, I will look someone in the face and tell them I did what I thought was right. If you succeed by doing what you think is right you get enormous satisfaction. By the same token, if you fail in doing what you feel is right then you only have yourself to blame.

If I started picking sides to avoid confrontations and just tried to keep players happy, then the bottom line would be that if things went wrong it's not all down to me. I would much prefer to know it was my decision rather than put a brave face on and pretend it was my doing when, really, it was not. As a result, I don't have hang ups, and on the back of that I avoid any major confrontations with any individual.

Players who come knocking on my door looking for reassurances are kidding themselves a bit. It is easy for anyone to come in after we have lost a game and say: "I should have been in the team." I understand that. But, as I have said, when it comes to transfers or picking teams I don't worry what people may think or say. I believe my decision is the correct one.

If I start chewing things over in my mind and think about the problems which could crop up, I would get nowhere. I have to dismiss all that, walk away for five minutes, if necessary, and then come back and select the team that I believe in. It is similar when it comes to transfers. I am very clear about what should be done and I am brave enough to back my judgement because, even if I am wrong, then at least I have done it the way I feel is right and proper.

So while there were some quite controversial departures in my first few months at the club, I felt I was doing the right thing, even though I was gambling by weakening the team quicker than perhaps I needed to, quicker than I should have been. Looking back, it has to be one of the biggest gambles I have ever taken as a manager, and I have to admit it almost put me in a situation which might have resulted in my not being here at the club today. But months on I am pleased that I had the guts to do it.

As far as bringing in new faces was concerned I needed to get the ball rolling and I did so by making Ian Taylor my first Villa signing. Again, questions were asked when I bought Ian. People did not think there was too much wrong with a midfield which included Houghton, Parker and Richardson. But I maintained from day one that I wanted my team to play a mobile game.

It is amazing how people have always misconstrued that, by thinking it is the long ball game. It isn't, and I think, months on, Ian has shown what I mean by mobility. He is a player who can get up and down the pitch, penalty box to penalty box, and slip in behind opposition defences. He can be quicker than the opposition.

Credit to Houghton, Richardson and Parker, their strengths were to keep the ball, and in Kevin's case winning the ball and keeping it simple. But I don't think you could call any of them what I describe as a box-to-box player, who could get beyond opposition defences and then get back to help in defence, thanks to enthusiasm, pace and the ability to keep going.

For all I look for mobility from players, technique is also high up the order of priorities as far as I am concerned. Ian has those assets. He was a player I had tried to sign for a long time and actually watched him very closely when I was still in charge at Leicester. He had only just moved to Sheffield Wednesday from Port Vale after being out of contract at Vale Park. I watched him again a few weeks before I signed him. He was asked to operate as a right-winger that day and, to be fair, he looked like a fish out of water. I could see he was not enjoying the role and, personally, I always regarded him as a central-midfield player who loved to run up and down the middle of the park and covered the ground unbelievably well.

It was strange, really, because I speak to Trevor Francis quite a lot. Trevor was manager at Hillsborough at that time and during one of our conversations he told me he was concerned that his side were having problems scoring goals. At the same time, he was having trouble buying a striker with the money he had available.

He mentioned Guy Whittingham to me, and although Guy was around the first team action at the time I had players like Dean Saunders, Dalian Atkinson and young Graham Fenton who were in front of him. So, in effect, Trevor had someone who I wanted in Ian, and I had someone who suited his requirements in Guy. At the time, both Trevor and I needed to do something to get out of trouble so we felt the deal might do us both a bit of good, even though we were losing players we would have been perfectly happy to keep.

It is often the case that, deep down, a manager would like to keep a certain player but knows by letting him go he can spark off a bit of transfer business which can be even more beneficial, long-term. I have to admit that when I first arrived at Villa there were players I would have rather sold than Guy. He was a smashing lad who worked hard and was well known to my coach, John Gregory. It was John who bought Guy out of the Army and gave him his chance at Portsmouth. So there was every chance that John might have got even more out of Guy than he had already shown at Villa.

Trevor and I agreed the deal although, at the time, he was also very keen to sign Paul McGrath as part of the package. Initially, I had left Paul out of my side for a spell and was very concerned for him. I thought long and hard about letting him go to Wednesday, perhaps thinking it would have been in his best interests. Thankfully, in the end, I decided not to part with him because during the following 18 months Macca proved to be one of my most consistent players.

There was speculation in a couple of newspapers at the time that Paul was on his way out of Villa but I just dismissed it, as you some-times have to in my job. So although Trevor would dearly liked to have taken Macca, it was finally agreed that Ian should join us and Guy should move to Hillsborough. Getting Ian into Villa Park was very important to me and I think he showed in his first game what a good signing he was going to be. He impressed on his debut at Arsenal, then marked his first game in front of our supporters by scoring in the 3-0 victory over Chelsea.

That was a very special day for Ian, who had been a lifelong Villa supporter. Coming out and scoring in front of the Holte End on his home debut is something he will probably remember for ever. But, generally, swap deals are always difficult to negotiate because all it needed was for either Ian, or Guy, to say he didn't want to move and the whole thing would have broken down. The signing of Ian rekindled my thoughts that Villa followers wanted me to do well but were, perhaps, questioning what I was doing.

There I was, bringing in someone who had basically been a reserve team player at Sheffield Wednesday for three months. So people were bound to look at the deal and think to themselves that they hoped it would turn out right for my sake. That was the feedback I got at the time. Even the chairman raised his eyebrows a bit although, in fairness to him, he always asks the type of questions the supporters would – for instance, is this lad genuinely better than what we have already?

Mr Ellis was keen to know my opinion on that, and all I can say is that I have always been positive in my thoughts about players I sign. Ian was one I was very positive about, although early on I am sure a lot of people were asking: "Ian who? Is he really going to keep Kevin Richardson or Ray Houghton out of the team?"

We were in the bottom four of the Premiership at the time and supporters were looking to me to buy players who would get us out of trouble. But as a manager I felt I was being brave enough not to think just short term but also to look that year or two on. The only thought I had in my head when I became Villa manager was to keep the club in the Premiership. But at the same time I wanted to make signings who I thought would become even better players as time progressed.

My next two signings were Tommy Johnson and Gary Charles, who joined us the day before we played at Barnsley in the third round of the FA Cup in early January, 1995. Again, questions were asked because I had gone out and spent £2.9m on two guys from Derby County, a club desperate to get into the Premiership at that time but were failing, despite their own huge outlay on players. A lot of us who watched Derby knew there was something there and subsequently a lot of the players Arthur Cox brought together moved on for big money. Not just Tommy and Gary, but also the likes of Paul Kitson, Craig Short and Mark Pembridge.

I sold Kitson to Derby when I was at Leicester. I knew that he, along with Gary and Tommy, were talented players. But when I went out and bought Gary and Tommy they proved to be very quiet lads when they first joined us. I mentioned earlier that I had inherited a bunch of players who could create a lot of noise off the field, so I think my two new signings found it all a bit intimidating. That made it very hard for them to settle with us during the opening few weeks.

Once more there were raised eyebrows after I had spent £2.9m on the pair of them, yet neither was a first team regular. Gary, in particular, found himself sitting on the sidelines, while Earl Barrett played in the right-back position. Earl was a very popular player at Villa and I quite liked him. But until Everton came in for him I could see him playing as a centre-back in my long-term planning, so that was one of the reasons why I wanted to bring in Gary. I never regarded Earl as the most confident of players going forward in possession, as I wanted a full-back to operate.

Earl was a good athlete, had good technique, but wasn't the bravest in that final one-third of the field, whereas Gary was more natural as an attacking full-back. But people at the time were looking at Earl as a solid defender, certainly one of the fittest players in the team, and perhaps wondering why I had brought in Gary at all. But some tend to forget that Gary had played for England at senior level and was a genuine talent, even though a few things had not gone right for him.

Similarly, Tommy had good pedigree. He had played at England under-21 level and showed he was always capable of scoring goals. He will always miss chances, but the one thing that impressed me about him was the fact that, even if he was having a bad spell, he would never disappear out of a game. The day I signed Tommy I told him he might end up playing a different role to the one he thought he was best at.

He looked at me a bit strangely but he wanted to join Villa, so at the time he didn't ask too many questions. But I could always see him as the guy who could go in and play in the spare role just behind the two main strikers. It took me a lot longer than I thought to convince Tommy that was his best position. But now, whenever I ask him to play in any other position than that free role just behind the front men, I can see in his face that he would much rather be operating in the position he has become accustomed to, because he has adjusted to it so well.

But when I signed them they both had their problems because they had not been signed from a Premiership club. People could not see them as players who were going to make the big impact we were looking for, there and then. But once again that was me being brave enough to say to myself: Give it time, it will work. All I have got to do is get us through this season and just make sure we are still in the Premiership at the end of it all.

As I said, the day after Tommy and Gary joined us we went to Barnsley in the FA Cup. I left Richardson and Houghton out of the side that day, with Taylor playing in midfield. So that was when my own team was beginning to take shape and it was pleasing that we went to Oakwell, played exceptionally well, and won 2-0 with goals from Dean Saunders and Dwight Yorke.

In fact, January went so well for me that as transfer deadline day approached I felt we were in a position where I could change things even more. But I guess, as things turned out, I got a bit of a false impression.

My final signing during that spell was Alan Wright, who moved on deadline day from Blackburn Rovers. Once again the inevitable questions were asked because I already had Steve Staunton who had established himself in the left-back position – and when people first saw Alan their reaction was that he was too small. Over the years he must have had that thrown at him hundreds of times. People threw it at me lots of times, that he was far too small to make any real impact in the team.

Once more I was buying a player who had had to content himself with reserve team football for a few months. Again, the chairman began asking the inevitable questions. Credit to the chairman, he has a knack of knowing what the supporters are thinking and was asking the questions on their behalf. But I told him I wanted the player and he backed me 100 per cent.

I return to the word pedigree. I remember Alan playing for Blackpool against Darlington as a 17-year-old and, even then, he was miles ahead of anyone else on the pitch. He became available at Blackburn because Kenny Dalglish had brought in Graeme Le Saux, who subsequently went on to establish himself at England level before his unfortunate accident. But I have spoken to Blackburn manager Ray Harford several times since and I know for a fact he would love to still have Alan at Ewood Park.

If Ray had been in charge at the time I am sure I would not have been allowed to sign Alan. Yet, in many respects, since he joined us Alan has been a revelation. People tend to underestimate him when they first see him, basically because of his size. It is a strange thing to say but that is a fact. In my opinion he is as gifted a player as we have at the club. He passes the ball as well as anyone and he strikes it better than most.

Because of his size, people worry about his aerial and heading ability, but he jumps unbelievably well and throughout the whole of last season not too many players got the better of him. Personally, I was very pleased with the signing of Alan because I knew that I now had two quality, left-sided players in my squad in him and Steve Staunton.

Injury problems did not really allow Steve to show me what his best position was but I think even Steve would concede that Alan has been a revelation since joining Villa. He cost me £900,000 and I know that in today's market I would have no chance of buying anyone of similar quality at that sort of price. It may have taken a bit of time but I think there is no doubt Alan has now convinced everyone he was a very good buy for the club. I was delighted when he agreed to sign a new four-year contract with us during the summer, which should guarantee that he will be at Villa Park until at least the year 2000.

Ironically, Alan's debut was against West Ham at home when we lost 2-0. The result was a major disappointment and gave us a hint of the problems we were going to have during the run-in to the end of the season, just at a time when we thought we had got ourselves out of trouble.

Chapter Six

The Dodgy Dozen

There have been certain events in my career that I hope have served to make me a better manager. Inevitably, some of the moments have not been particularly pleasant, but I would like to think I have learned from them.

Perhaps the most vivid example of a learning process during my time at Villa came on the evening of February 22, 1995, when we entertained my former club, Leicester City, in a Premiership match in front of nearly 21,000 supporters at Villa Park. It is a game I am sure many of the Villa fans remember only too well. It will certainly be etched in my memory for a very long time to come.

I still recall, as if it was yesterday, glancing up from the dug-out at the clock inside Villa Park and thinking to myself that there were only about 15 minutes of the match remaining. We were cruising through the game with a healthy 4-1 lead. The victory I anticipated at that stage would have taken us beyond 40 points for the season, and well on the way to Premiership safety.

I always felt we needed 50 points to be absolutely sure of staying up. When any new campaign begins, you can bet that every manager in the League will think that if his team can reach 50 points, then they will have no fears of being relegated. Three points against Leicester would have left us with the fairly easy task of needing just another nine from our remaining dozen outings to reach the target.

Remember, the night we played Leicester we were actually up in ninth place in the Premiership and there was still an outside chance of us securing a place in Europe for the following season.

Franz Carr and Dalian Atkinson were on the substitutes' bench for the Leicester game, along with Nigel Spink. Everything had gone so well for the first 75 minutes that I decided I would give both Franz and Dalian a run-out for the final 15 minutes or so. I told them both to start warming up. But within three minutes Leicester scored to make in 4-2.

Even then I did not worry for one second that anything would go wrong, not just in that game, but in the 12 that we still had to play to complete the season. So I put the two subs on, Franz against his former club, and Dalian taking part in his first senior game since our Coca-Cola Cup defeat by Crystal Palace nearly three months earlier. Suddenly, in the space of 12 minutes, our three-goal lead vanished and the game ended all square at 4-4.

At the time I did not admit it publicly, but I have to say now that for those 12 minutes I just switched off, probably more so than at any other time as a football manager. I genuinely thought that at 4-1 up the game had been won, we were into the 40's as far as points were concerned, and the threat of relegation was no longer an issue to concern us. With 12 games and 12 minutes of the season still remaining, I remember thinking to myself that my first aim as Villa manager had been achieved, we would be staying in the Premiership.

I have to say that for spells we were absolutely outstanding against Leicester, and at one stage I thought we would emulate our performance against Wimbledon two games earlier and score another seven goals. But those last 12 minutes became a nightmare. The two substitutions I made were poor ones. I just wanted to give Franz a little run against the club he had left to join us, and at the time I thought it would be nice for Dalian to have a taste of the action, after being out injured for so long.

But now, as I look back on that eventful game, I realise there was one hell of a lesson to be learned, as far as I was concerned. I will never again be so blasé, or even flippant, about seeing my team in such a commanding position, and seemingly on their way to an easy victory. I promise I will never allow myself to switch off like that again and not concentrate fully on my job for all the 90 minutes. I suppose of all the sides we might have been playing that night, it just had to be Leicester!

There was a feeling of shock, rather than one of disappointment, in the dressing room afterwards. I did not analyse our performance too much at the time, although I realise now that we were so static for their last three goals, it was unbelievable. I had turned off, and clearly my players had as well.

Even though we had to settle for a draw that February night and stayed just under the 40-point mark, we still had 12 games to go to the end of the season. Although there is no such thing as an easy game, I looked at our programme and felt we would be able to pick up sufficient points from the remainder and avoid relegation without too many worries. In fact, we never really recovered from that dreadful last 12 minutes against Leicester, and the rest of the season turned out to be a real dogfight for survival. After a dodgy dozen minutes, we were in for a dodgy dozen games.

Our next outing was against Newcastle United up at St James' Park. For the first 45 minutes we played some really good football but lost in 90 minutes, 3-1. That was the match in which Barry Venison scored his first goal for Newcastle. When he was about 25 or 30 yards from goal there was actually a shout from our dug-out for him to shoot, because we thought he would hit it high, or wide. His effort flew into the top corner of the net. I am sure it is a goal he remembers very well. He certainly left a few of us with egg on our faces.

Andy Townsend levelled the score with an equally spectacular goal, and we went in 1-1 at half time genuinely feeling we had a good chance of getting something out of the game. But in the end we were beaten by two pieces of superb individual brilliance from Peter Beardsley.

There is one sentence I always try to avoid as a manager and that is: "We played well today, even though we lost."

To me there is absolutely no satisfaction in doing that, or saying it. I am very much a result-orientated manager and I cringe if I hear other managers claim they were unlucky to lose after playing so well.

Sometimes even I begin the sentence, but try to shut up before I have said it all. Yet when I look back at some of those games towards the end of the 1994-95 season, I have to say that we were playing well, but we were not winning.

I always worry when that begins to happen. I can look back over my years as a scout and a coach and recall watching scores of games where teams were playing well, but the ruthless streak that helps make winners had deserted them. Successful teams win games in different ways. Sometimes they dominate throughout, but on other occasions they grind out victories, often when they are playing badly. Sometimes you just sense that even though they are a little below par, once they edge ahead they are there to stay.

We came up against a team with that gritty determination and mentality in our next game when we entertained Blackburn Rovers. Once again we played well and were a match for them for most of the game. But after Alan Shearer put them ahead I just knew they were going to win 1-0. There would be no way back for us.

Each season there is usually one team who sets the example for the rest. That season it was Blackburn's turn, and they were a great role model to a lot of teams. They really believed in winning matches, and hung on in all sorts of situations.

There was an enormous desire in the Blackburn camp to be successful in whatever manner it took. Although Manchester United have enjoyed tremendous success these past few seasons, playing bright, attractive football, I was full of admiration for Blackburn that season because of their determination not to lose games. It was that resolve that enabled them to fulfil Jack Walker's dream and win the Premiership.

Meanwhile, we were still very much involved in trying to get enough points to stave off relegation, and even though we had managed just one point from three games, there was no real cause for panic. I looked at our next series of games, against Coventry City, West Ham United, Ipswich Town, Crystal Palace and Chelsea – all teams, like ourselves, struggling at the wrong end of the table – and I genuinely felt we were capable of winning all five.

We had just come up against two good sides, played well, but lost.

Perhaps I dismissed those defeats as just something that happens in football every so often. Dare I say, we had played well, even though we had lost both. For the one and only time in my life I found myself saying the very sentence I hated, perhaps looking for an excuse for the fact that we had nothing to show for decent performances against Newcastle and Blackburn.

We looked at the next five matches coming up and were confident that, even if we did not win all of them, we would pick up sufficient points to erase all our problems. As we went into the game against Coventry, I remember thinking to myself that Dean Saunders would maybe score a couple of goals and pull us through – or Dalian would come off the subs' bench again, go on one of those runs he was capable of, and score a special goal.

As I look back, with a certain amount of embarrassment I have to say, I realise I had switched off. I had adopted a far too casual approach, thinking to myself that everything would turn out all right. I often tell my players in the dressing room not to wait for things to happen but to go out and make them happen. Do not wait for the ball to come to you, go and find it. Yet I had abandoned that approach myself. I was still working hard at my job but I was just sitting there, expecting us to get out of trouble.

For whatever reason, the relief valve in me had opened up far too early. I have mentioned that my only aim during that first season was to keep Villa in the Premiership, and I thought the task had already been achieved. There was a false sense of security which had been self-inflicted. From me, through my coaching staff and down to the first team squad, everyone had the same casual approach.

There is no way we should have been sucked back into the relegation battle. Even after the draw against Leicester we were still ninth in the table and our results during January had earned me the Manager of the Month award. But now we were about to take on Midland neighbours Coventry, which meant a return to Villa Park for Ron Atkinson. That was not a problem to me, even though Sky TV obviously felt there was some significance in it, because they decided to screen it as their live Monday night match.

There were no hard feelings between Ron and myself. I met up with him, wished him well, and that was about it. I am not the sort to invite managers into my office for a drink after games, whether it is Ron or anyone else. Ron was tremendously well-received by the Villa supporters, which I thought was superb. I remember Sky TV pundit Andy Gray saying just before the game that Ron was the best manager he had worked for, and I was one of the best players he had ever played with, which was flattering for both of us.

So I had no hang-ups about Ron's return for a game in which we again played well, should have won, but didn't. In the end we had to settle for a point from the goalless draw. But it was another of those games where I was saying to myself afterwards that we had played well enough, so there was no problem. Yet there we were, gradually falling back down the slippery slope, and I was still not fully grasping the seriousness of the situation – still not able to take off the blinkers and realise the desperate position we were dropping back into.

I have always prided myself in being able to see these types of situations unfolding. But, in all honesty, on this occasion I just could not see what was going on. Maybe I was kidding myself, I don't really know. But I was adopting the attitude that there was no need to worry, we would be all right.

Our next opponents were West Ham, a club I always did fairly well against during my playing days. It was also a third successive home game for us and I was in no doubt that we would pick up maximum points. How wrong I was. We lost the game 2-0 and for the first time the alarm bells began to ring. Before the match West Ham were below us in the table and it was one of those proverbial six-pointers. Once again we did not play badly, but they had a shot in the first half and scored, then did the same in the second half. The defeat sent us tumbling down to 15th in the table. We had dropped down six places in less than a month.

Even more alarming was the fact that we were not taking points off teams who were in similar trouble to us. Sure, we managed a draw against Coventry, but instead of an anticipated three points off West Ham we ended up with nothing. Instead of moving well clear of them in the fight for survival we were right there alongside them, fighting for Premiership survival.

All of a sudden we were a pale shadow of the side who had gone out so confidently throughout the month of January and drawn at Leeds, then strung together victories over Barnsley in the FA Cup, and QPR, Nottingham Forest and Tottenham Hotspur, in quick succession, in the Premiership. Our bravery had disappeared. In a very short space of time there had been a complete reversal of team belief and approach to games.

By selling the likes of Richardson, Houghton and Parker, I had laid my cards on the table. I am sure there was a feeling within some parts of the dressing room that, whether we survived or not, it did not particularly matter to some of the players, because they thought they would be next to leave. I had unwittingly created seeds of doubt in people's minds. There was a degree of uncertainty in the dressing room that was beginning to backfire.

Transfer deadline day had passed, so they knew they were safe until the end of the season. But then what? Instead of lifting my players for the vital run-in to the end of the season, I realise now that I had done something that had only served to dampen their spirits. Obviously it was not right, otherwise the results would have been much better.

I go back to the fact that it is one of the most difficult jobs in management, to try to change things around in mid-season. I had been forced to dabble in the transfer market and, as a result, players had begun to look over their shoulders wondering if they would be next to go once the season was over. Whatever the problem, there was definitely something missing from within the team that had been there only a month or so earlier.

There was a real problem, but there was nothing I could do about it. There could be no more moves into the transfer market until the summer. I had what I had. I knew I just had to get on with it the best I could and hope that things would eventually turn out favourably. If ever there was a time when I needed a bit of luck it was in our next match, away to Ipswich, another team deep in relegation trouble.

The performance at Portman Road was undoubtedly our worst since I took over as manager. Yet we scraped the points, courtesy of an own-goal by Chris Swailes in the very last minute. Afterwards there was the feeling in the dressing room that because we had played so badly yet won through a fluky goal, everything was going to be all right after all. We had three very valuable points, so I felt there was no point in charging into the dressing room and telling everyone how poorly we had played.

I thought it was best to try to keep everyone happy, despite the under-current of unrest that clearly existed. I was, perhaps, as low profile as I have ever been, not just in the dressing room, but even back at the training ground when we began preparing for our next match against Crystal Palace at Selhurst Park. There seemed little point in handing out a verbal lashing for our display against Ipswich – after all, we had picked up a victory. Once more the feelings were within me that we would escape, everything would turn out for the best. But, deep down, I knew that things were still far from right.

Incidentally, the goal at Portman Road was the first one we had managed in four games, and little did I know at the time that we would then go another four agonising matches without finding the back of the net.

The match at Crystal Palace was another massive one for us, in terms of if we had won it would have seen us clear of trouble, for sure. But if Lady Luck had smiled on us with the own-goal victory at Portman Road, then luck was definitely against us at Selhurst Park. You may recall it was the game where Dalian actually scored a perfectly good goal that was not allowed. At the time, it was suggested the ball had not crossed the line, but television evidence later proved beyond doubt it was a goal that should have stood.

So instead of three points from the game at Palace we had to settle for one, from a goalless draw. If I was looking for some consolation it was the fact that we actually played better than Palace that night, in sharp contrast to our previous performance at Ipswich.

The match at Selhurst Park also gave me the opportunity to take another close look at a certain Gareth Southgate, a Palace player at the time. He played ever so well against us and I thought to myself, there and then, that he was the sort of player I would be looking to sign once the season was over.

So although we had to settle for a draw at Palace, at least some good came out of it. Gareth's display had pushed him to near the top of my wanted list. That helped temper the fact that we left South London for the long trip home knowing we should have won, but had to settle for a point because a perfectly good goal had been ruled out.

We were soon back in London for a meeting with Chelsea, and just three days later we faced the prospect of taking on Arsenal at Villa Park. We lost 1-0 at Stamford Bridge in a very poor game. They scored an early goal on a pitch, I have to say, that was very bumpy, and although we had a bit of the play we never looked like scoring. We were incapable of putting any real pressure on them. We went into the match with Chelsea below us in the table, but came out of it with them up alongside us.

So we had been dragged even deeper into trouble by the fact that instead of putting daylight between them and us, we had allowed them to close the gap. That really was a horrible day for all of us. Afterwards, the dressing room was a quiet as I have ever seen one. Everyone was obviously very aware that things were very wrong. No-one seemed prepared to say anything and the silence was deafening.

That made the game against Arsenal even more important in terms of getting the right result. As it was a home game, I decided we should go out and have a real go at them. I wanted my players to get at their defence as much as we possibly could. But the fact that we had adopted an attacking approach meant that we simply could not defend as well. I kept trying to be positive to get the victory we needed, but it turned out to be the worst defeat we could possibly have suffered at the time – 4-0 at the hands of Arsenal, in front of a crowd of more than 32,000 who were willing us to win and steer clear of trouble.

It had taken a long time, but that defeat suddenly woke us all up to the fact that we were under pressure, we could get relegated. That was the day that players began voicing their concern in the dressing room. In some respects it was a relief to me that big-name players were finally talking to each other about the situation in a loud manner – not violent, not nasty, but in a positive manner. They were saying to one another that we had just four games left, and if we did not sort ourselves out very quickly then we were facing the drop.

There was still time to do something about it, but we could not wait for it to happen. We had to go out and make it happen. It was no good waiting for other teams around us to lose to save our skins. Our destiny was in our own hands. From ninth off the top we had dropped down to 16th place and we going the wrong way fast. We had been sucked right back into the relegation battle and it was up to us to get out of it.

After the defeat by Arsenal I knew I had to play three centre backs to try to tighten up the defence. We could not afford to lose any more games by a four-goal margin. Despite the fact that everyone in the team was now very aware of the dangers of relegation, we again failed to take anything from our next match, against Leeds at Elland Road. But even though we had not improved our chances of staying up, and indeed had dropped another two places down the table, a lot of good came out of the game as well.

That was the occasion I played Dwight Yorke up front on his own, with Dean Saunders operating on the right side. I have to say, that as an out-and-out front man, Dwight was fantastic, absolutely outstanding. He showed me how he could use his strength to hold the ball up and bring team mates into the play. I knew that day that I had discovered something long-term for the club.

Here was someone who was better than the players he had always followed in the pecking order, the likes of Dean Saunders and Dalian Atkinson. It is perhaps unfair to Deano to say Yorkie was better. Let's just say different. There was a quality in Dwight that people had maybe seen but never really given the opportunity. I knew from that day that whatever happened, even if we were relegated, I had found the person who was going to be my main striker.

We played quite well against Leeds. However, Mark Bosnich got sent off near the end for a second bookable offence. Then Carlton Palmer scored for Leeds very late on, and I remember just sinking to my knees in disbelief. Inevitably, the photographers were on hand to capture the moment. There I was in the newspapers the following morning, down on my knees with everyone suggesting we were on our way to the First Division.

But the good things to come out of the game were Dwight's showing as a front man, and the fact that three central defenders was the system to go for. In football you tend to be remembered for your last few games, so as we left Elland Road most folk had forgotten that a few weeks earlier we had been ninth from top. All our supporters were thinking about now was the fact that we were 18th in the table, and with four to be relegated there was no more room for error.

There were lots more question marks being placed against me, and whether I was the right man for the job after all. That was understandable because everything in this game is a mood swing. All the majority of fans are interested in is what is happening at present, not what has gone on in the past. That made me dig deep on my reserves. I thought about all the bad experiences I had suffered during my time in the game, which helped produce an inner strength to have the belief to get through these traumatic times.

We scrambled a 1-1 draw in our next outing, at home to Manchester City, thanks to a goal from Ugo Ehiogu. It was only a point, but it was a very important one. It meant the four teams below us had to do something to close the gap. Then it was Liverpool at home, and that proved to be a terrific day for us.

To me that was the day when the Villa fans decided they needed to turn out in their thousands and give us every bit of backing they could muster to try to help the club stay up. We responded with a fantastic display, with Dwight, playing in a striker's role, scoring both goals in the 2-0 victory. It underlined the belief I had in Dwight to play in that position, and suddenly there was hope again.

In time of trouble team spirit sometimes shines through, and this was an occasion when it did. Whatever their individual futures might be, the players showed me that day that they did not want to get relegated.

Everyone sensed that if we could get out of trouble we would all learn from the experience. Personally, I was just hell bent on surviving, and then making sure that this type of thing would never happen to me again. I knew if we survived I would do better the following season. I always say: 'Look, listen and learn'. Never sit in the middle of a room and not know what is going on behind you. When I go into a room I like to position myself so that I can see everything that is going on.

Yet, I suppose, in the run-in to the end of the season I had not positioned myself well enough to see what was going on around me, and it was a lesson I was determined to learn. Although I talk about the last 12 games of the season, in fact, the last four of the season were not that bad. I thought we played well, but there was that period of eight matches when we were dire. For me, there was a lifetime of learning in those games. By the time the last four games came round, I felt I had put it right, but there was still a chance I had acted too late.

Fortunately, the Liverpool result provided the perfect boost we were looking for. It meant that we went into the last game of the season, at Norwich, knowing we had to avoid defeat to be safe. Even if we did lose Palace had to get three points from their trip to Newcastle to overtake us. It still proved to be quite an eventful day, because I sent coaches Tony McAndrew and Kevin MacDonald up to St James' Park armed with a mobile phone each.

Personally, I hate mobile phones in and around the dressing room and training ground, and would willingly ban them. But that was an occasion when I was glad they had been invented. As we played Norwich I had a mobile phone in the dug-out at Carrow Road. Every 10 minutes or so, either Tony or Kevin was on to me, keeping me informed on how Palace were getting on.

Those 90 minutes would have been tough to get through had I not known what was going on at St James' Park. Gradually, the information came through that Newcastle were in front. Their game finished just before ours, so even before the final whistle had gone blown at Norwich I knew we were safe. I have a photograph taken of me that day, sitting on a wall at Norwich with a big smile on my face. I had just heard the news that Palace had lost and Villa were still in the Premiership.

Although I was smiling, I have to admit I thought I would have been a lot happier than I actually was. Sure, I was pleased, but there and then I had to face up to the fact that survival was not a real achievement. Winning is the name of the game, and even in the euphoria that surrounded our dressing room that afternoon, I sat down and told myself to make sure this never happened to me again.

On the way down to the dressing room after the final whistle, the chairman came up to me and gave me a big hug. He had been so nervous beforehand, but now the relief on his face was there for all to see. It made me realise just how much Premiership survival meant to him. Probably a lot more than any of you can really imagine.

I suppose the mood in the dressing room was one of: "Well, we knew we were going to be all right." In some of the players I could see a bit of an image thing going on. I knew that some of the guys would never have got on with me and worked for me. Even though we were safe I knew my dressing room was not right. I did not travel back on the team coach from Norwich with the players. To be honest, I just wanted to get away from them for a while. Heather had driven down to watch the game and I travelled home with her.

My mind was already racing as I thought just how much work I had to do to transform Villa from a side who had only just avoided relegation into one capable of winning a piece of silverware the following season. There was no time to waste, I had to think and act accordingly. People were still asking whether I was the right man for the job, but in my own mind I now knew I was.

I have been asked a number of times if I would have offered my resignation if we had been relegated. The answer to that is, no, I would not . I made a statement when I joined Villa that I did not want to be a failure. But because the club were in trouble when I joined them, then I would have wanted the opportunity to have brought them back, had the worst happened.

You may remember that the day I heard Ron Atkinson had been sacked as Villa manager I was over in Majorca looking to buy an apartment. It was something Heather and I had wanted for several years, and as a result of us staying in the Premiership we travelled back to Majorca shortly afterwards and fulfilled our ambition by buying a nice apartment in Puerto Pollensa, where we still often go if I feel we need to get away from it all for a few days.

Chapter Seven

In The Summertime

As soon as the last ball of the 1994-95 season had been kicked I knew the time had come to make further changes. I was fully aware that at least one change would be forced on me. Soon after I arrived at Villa I discovered that Dean Saunders had a clause in his contract allowing him to leave the club for a certain fee if an offer from abroad was made for him.

I realised at the time not many people were aware of the option he had, but in fairness, players' contracts are personal matters and should not be made public. In many respects too many details are available to too many people these days, which causes unnecessary problems for mangers when it comes to trying to run a happy ship. It really can be quite a headache.

Dean and I had spoken about his clause on several occasions and, credit to him, he had been open enough to tell me that he did have this desire to go and try something different on the Continent. So I was always aware of the fact that if an offer came in from abroad I would have to resign myself to losing his services.

When Dean moved from Liverpool, I dare bet Villa got one hell of a good deal on him. He probably had to forsake all sorts of perks that he had at Anfield. But the perk he received for signing for Villa was the fact that when he was into his 30's he would be allowed to move to Europe for a set fee.

Interest quickly became apparent, so it was inevitable that Dean would soon be on his way. I knew he was very popular with the supporters, and questions would be asked as to why I was letting him go without putting up more of a fight. But it was one of those things that had to happen, and I realised that if that was what he really wanted to do then there was little point in trying to persuade him otherwise. I was also aware that Dean would be a difficult act to follow, not just because of his popularity with supporters, but also because he was such a bubbly person around the dressing room, a real laugh-a-minute character.

So I began looking for a replacement striker, and I really was covering all aspects. During that summer we were linked with the likes of Les Ferdinand, Dennis Bergkamp and Chris Armstrong. The chairman and I were being kept very well informed on what was going on in the transfer market and it became public knowledge that we made a move to sign Ferdinand.

Les travelled to Villa Park for the day to meet the chairman and myself, and I have to say that we had a super day with him. It provided me with a fascinating insight into transfer dealings at that top end of the scale. We were talking about a £6m deal, which is quite phenomenal money when you sit down and think about it.

A lot of people tend to dismiss such figures these days. I often get stopped in the street by punters, who ask me if I am going to buy so-and-so, because his club only want £3m. I think, ONLY £3m? That is an awful lot of cash as far as I am concerned. Folk reckon it is amazing if someone wins that amount on the lottery yet, when you talk about transfer fees, similar sorts of figures appear to mean very little to most people.

Even before we talked to Les we knew Newcastle were interested in him, and through the grapevine we were aware that that was probably the move the player wanted. But the chairman and I had discussed the situation at great length, and both agreed that if we had a number one choice, a guy who would guarantee goals in the Premiership, then Les was the man. We knew the fee we would have to pay would prevent us from doing other deals, but we felt the risk of that was worthwhile.

Les had a good look around Villa Park, and I formed the opinion that he was very impressed by what he saw. In fairness, though, we had just had a disappointing season and Newcastle appeared to be on the way up. Les perhaps looked on us as a very big club but was unsure as to how we would do in future. So in the end he opted for the move to St James' Park.

That led me to sit down with the chairman and express my opinion that in view of the season we had just had, maybe we were not in the position to persuade that type of player to join us. So I began doing my homework elsewhere, keeping in touch with many managers about the availability of players. What has since become well documented is that I also began checking videos of some of the leading Continental goalscorers. I have had a bit of criticism about signing a player after only watching a video of him, but that is the modern way of checking out players without having to travel here, there and everywhere.

I actually went over to Italy a few times that summer to look at several foreign strikers playing in Serie A of the Italian League, but I kept coming back to the video I had of a young Bosnian Serb striker, Savo Milosevic. Everything about his play impressed me – how much he was involved in games, and the goals he scored.

So I began finding out as much about Savo as I could, which included long chats with Terry Venables, who had seen the lad play first hand. Terry and other managers in Europe were providing glowing tributes and I knew a number of top Italian clubs were anxious to sign Savo. That was one thing playing on my mind. I was also thinking about other areas of the team which needed to be strengthened.

I wanted to, maybe, bring in someone who would complement the midfield play of Ian Taylor and Andy Townsend. Through the grapevine we had heard that Gareth Southgate was going to become available. So the names of Southgate and Milosevic were very much in my thinking. I had made it clear to the chairman that Gareth was a player I very much wanted. During a conversation, almost out of the blue, between Mr Ellis and Palace chairman Ron Noades, a fee was agreed for Gareth which I felt was a good deal.

At the time it was suggested we had paid £2.5m for Gareth, but if my memory serves me right the actual figure was £2.25m which, I am sure, everyone will agree was an excellent bit of business for a player who has now gone on to establish himself, not only for us, but also at international level for England.

The transfer itself could hardly have been easier. After we had been given permission to talk to him Gareth travelled up to Villa Park and spent the whole day looking around, not just at the ground, but at the Bodymoor Heath training centre as well. Gareth gave me the immediate impression he wanted to come to Villa – he was ready to join us – and by the end of a day's negotiations Gareth had agreed to sign. It was very unusual to conclude such a big-money transfer in such a short time.

After we had tied up all the loose ends, I told him that he would have to make his way home that evening, then be back in Birmingham first thing the following morning for a Press conference. But typical of Gareth, he was very well organised. He had brought a spare change of clothes and a packed bag with him in his car. He wanted to join us, but there again, so many other players in a similar situation would probably not even have thought about bringing a change of clothes, just in case.

Even I didn't expect things to go through so smoothly, or so quickly. When Gareth left home to talk to us that day he obviously had a good idea what he wanted to do, and I was delighted that we had brought in such a quality player. But while the negotiations with Gareth were taking place, in the quieter moments of the day I was still involved in talks with the chairman about Milosevic, a player who was going to cost us £3.5m from Partizan Belgrade.

After Gareth had signed I sat down again with the chairman and told him how much I wanted to sign Milosevic. I think he was on such a high after tying up the first deal that he got on the phone to Partizan officials and asked if we could fly over to meet them the following day. They agreed, so we booked two air tickets that night to fly out to a country which, at the time, was a war zone.

Looking back, it really was a fantastic day. One £2.25m deal had been completed, and now we were about to fly off to try to complete another deal worth a club record £3.5m. At the Southgate Press conference the next morning no one knew that the chairman and I just wanted to get things over with as quickly as possible so we could rush down to Heathrow Airport and jump on a plane bound for Belgrade.

It was only when we were up in the air that the chairman drew a deep breath, looked at me and said: "You do realise, don't you, that we are flying straight into a troubled area." We just looked at each other in astonishment when the realisation hit us both. As it happened, when we arrived in Belgrade the organisation was first class.

The security was unbelievable. We needed all sorts of documents to get into the country, but everything had been taken care of by the Partizan officials. We were whisked away from the airport to the Partizan ground and then began what I can only describe as hours and hours of negotiations.

We arrived at the ground at about 2.00pm, and from then on it was real cloak and dagger stuff. Their representatives, who spoke perfect English, kept leaving the room to have their private talks, and the chairman and I were doing the same.

And all this was going on after I had watched only a video of Savo. I would hardly say it was typical of me, but I guess it is as brave a step as I have ever undertaken in my years in management. But the minute I met Savo for the first time I knew there was a brightness and strength about him which impressed me, particularly for such a young man.

Agreement was finally reached at midnight, ten hours after talks had begun. I have already completed quite a few deals sitting alongside the chairman and seen him hold court and barter, but I have to say that in Belgrade he was at his brilliant best. There were serious moments, there was laughter and fun during the talks, but all the way through he was right at it.

We shook hands on the deal virtually as the clock struck midnight, then all went out for a meal to a superb restaurant in Belgrade. We arrived back to our hotel at about 3.30 in the morning. By 8.00am we were on our way back to the airport to jump on a plane bound for Heathrow.

Savo and his representatives were travelling with us so that he could have a look around Villa Park and see if he liked the place. He loved it - had his routine medical, and the deal was done. In a little more than 48 hours, the £6m I had lined up to buy Les Ferdinand had been spent bringing in Gareth and Savo. That evening the chairman again showed the enormous stamina he has by taking Savo and the Belgrade representatives out for a meal in Birmingham. I was absolutely shattered, so I just went straight home to bed.

The next morning Savo and the rest travelled back to Belgrade, and I knew that the next time he came to our country he could only do so with a work permit. That was never going to be a problem because of the fee involved and his pedigree as a player. He was only 21, but he was already a full Yugoslav international. Even so, the work permit seemed to take an age to come through. It did arrive, eventually, and Savo was my second big signing of the summer. Looking back, those 48 hours of activity involving Gareth and Savo will certainly take some matching.

It soon became public knowledge that we had signed this player from Partizan called Savo Milosevic but no one could really come up with much information about him, even though he was greatly admired in his own country, with pictures of him everywhere. I can only compare his popularity over there with that of Dwight Yorke back in Trinidad and Tobago, where he is affectionately known as King Dwight.

So there was this element of mystery surrounding Savo. What was he going to be like? Would he settle in this country? All the typical questions that supporters ask. Inevitably, the chairman was asking the same.

Although Savo took a bit of a time to settle into the English game, I think he began to show as the season progressed what a fine young player he is. It is worth remembering that when he joined us he was still only 21, and was coming to play in, arguably, one of the toughest Leagues in the world. He also knew very little of the English language, but he has done extremely well to speak it in such a short time. I am sure we are about to see him really come to the fore in the future.

After we had acquired both Gareth and Savo, it was fairly well documented at the time that I was looking for a central defender. I was trying to establish the backbone of the team and, having brought in a centre forward and a central midfield player, as everyone saw Gareth at the time, the next obvious target was a central defender. I was being linked with a variety of defenders, yet behind the scenes I had had several conversations with Mark McGhee, who was Leicester manager at the time, about Mark Draper.

Leicester did not really want to lose Draper. But out of the blue Mark McGhee rang me one day and asked if the player became available, would I still be interested in buying him. I said he knew I would be, so when I got the call I went straight to the chairman and told him the lad was available and I wanted to do the deal. In my mind I had selected Gareth as my midfield player, but I knew he was a very versatile player who could play at the back.

You know in your own mind that when a player of Draper's quality becomes available you just have to go for it. I have never revealed it before, but a lot of the transfer deal involving Draper was carried out while I was sitting in a hairdresser's chair in Nottingham. I always went to this particular place to get my hair cut by a guy who was absolutely football daft and a big Leicester City supporter.

I went in to have my hair cut this particular day and I told him that I had to keep my mobile telephone close by because I was expecting a call or two. Sure enough, the phone rang a couple of times, and even though my hairdresser walked away to give me a bit of privacy, as soon as he returned he started asking me if it was Draper I was trying to sign from his club. Although some of the initial work had been carried out the evening before, with faxes and the like travelling back and forth between Mark McGhee and myself, the deal was actually finalised while I was having my hair cut.

I guess it is pretty unique that a deal involving a player costing a very big fee of £3.25m should be carried out in such an unusual setting, with conversations taking place between myself and Martin George, Mark McGhee and Mark Draper, while I was getting my trim. The Draper deal changed the team planning I had in my mind. I realised that although Gareth had played the majority of his football at Crystal Palace as a midfielder, I believed he could adapt to a central defensive position in the new strategy I was drawing up.

The Draper deal was again very easy, considering such a big fee was involved. Deep down I knew that Mark would always be willing to sign for me after I became Villa manager. I signed him from Notts County when I was in charge at Leicester and he proved to be a terrific acquisition at Filbert Street. When I moved to Villa there was a lot of speculation that he would follow me and I received a lot of feedback from supporters suggesting he would be an ideal signing.

Although questions had been asked about some of my earlier signings, once Mark agreed to join us I sensed fans were beginning to sit up, take notice and agree that he was the type who would benefit the club. Initially, people were not sure about the Southgate deal, while Milosevic was the big mystery with everyone asking what was going on, bringing in a relatively unknown quantity, as far as this country was concerned.

But the arrival of Draper seemed to blow away the uncertainty. Suddenly, supporters sensed there really was something happening. Publicly, people thought I was creating healthy competition, with Townsend, Taylor, Draper and Southgate vying for the midfield places. They could see the new-look team beginning to take shape.

In the meantime Garry Parker moved to Leicester and we took Franz Carr. Leicester were looking for someone of Garry's midfield experience and I wanted a winger on our books, so the deals suited both clubs. As things turned out, Franz did not get much of a chance to prove himself, but he is a good sort to have around the dressing room and did well keeping an eye on the likes of Charles, Johnson and Draper, which is important for me.

Meanwhile, Garry did well at Leicester, playing his part in getting them back into the Premiership by winning the First Division play-off Final against Crystal Palace at Wembley. He was a player I could so easily have kept, but it was a case of the right deal coming along for both club and player.

When we began pre-season training the one thing that hit me first was the fact that, the way things were working out, I was not going to start the season with Shaun Teale as one of my central defenders. Shaun had been a fine servant to Villa, but I go back to the fact that it was all about a player at the wrong age not being in the first team.

There was interest from Tranmere and after he had talks with them the two clubs agreed a fee.

I thought a lot of Shaun, he was a smashing lad who would always give you 100 per cent once he pulled on a Villa shirt. But I emphasise, Shaun was allowed to go for his benefit more than anyone else's. Once I was playing Gareth in that position I knew he gave us something a bit different. He had more mobility than Shaun and was a different competitor. I remember a lot of people coming up to me and telling me not to sell Shaun because he and Paul Mcgrath had been the defensive rocks of the team.

But it was something I felt I had to do at the time. It would have been unfair on the player to keep him hanging around in the reserves instead of allowing him the chance to move on, accept a new challenge, and play regular first team football elsewhere. Also, there was the fact that if he had been languishing in the reserves then later in the season I probably would not have got the type of money that we sold him for. So it cut both ways.

Dalian Atkinson was something of a different issue. There was a problem with him pre-season, in as much as he had publicly stated that he wanted to leave Villa. He had got himself into that frame of mind, so I felt it was best that he did not even do pre-season training with us. I wanted to make a good, clean start, and because I actually got on very well with Dalian, I sat down with him and told him I realised he wanted to get away and I would help him any way I could.

But I also said to him that because his future at the time was unsettled I did not want him to take part in the pre-season build-up with the rest of the lads. Dalian was at ease with that. I know a lot of people did not have much time for him, but I genuinely liked him and, at times, felt he was a bit misunderstood. So although my decision not to let him train with the other players might have looked like a snub to him, actually, it was something we both agreed on.

Dalian had had a difficult time in the previous season, missing a lot of games through injury, and clubs were questioning whether they should sign him. There were bits of interest from other clubs, nothing definite, before Fenerbahçe of Turkey made a positive move. Turkey would probably not have been his first choice, but at least the move provided him with the opportunity to get away from the English game for a while and start afresh.

I always got the impression that the feelings about Dalian were very mixed. Some people always saw him as this guy who could score spectacular goals. Nothing wrong with that, at all. However, there was always this inconsistency in terms of what I was looking for. I needed people to be involved in the game all the time. I need a team which is perpetual motion, one which will work as much when the opposition have the ball as when we have it.

Those ingredients were a little lacking in Dalian's game. He was more of a power player, who could suddenly burst on to the scene, and cause problems to the opposition when he had the ball. But his style was not one of always being on the go, chasing around. Before anyone reminds me, I know I wasn't the type of player who chased around all afternoon. But I always felt my style suited the players around me. In any case the game has changed since my day, and I always maintain you cannot make a player into something that he is not.

That is why a manager buys certain players to play certain roles. It is all very well for people to say you should go out and buy so-and-so because he is a good player, or ask why have you left such a good player out of the team, but it is all about team pattern, and if things are not working then you have to be brave enough to do something about it. Unfortunately, I could never see Dalian falling into the style that I was trying to create.

With the new players I had brought in I could now see a definite pattern taking shape. Three centre-backs, two fairly adventurous full-backs, two or three mobile but extremely talented midfield men, then the option of either two quality strikers who want to be in the game a lot, or with someone playing in that spare role just behind them, the one I referred to last season as the Tommy Johnson role. My transfer dealings had finally given me something I felt would give provide the opportunity to stamp my way of playing on to the team.

As the season progressed, Steve Staunton found himself having a tough time with injuries. Although young Riccardo Scimeca occasionally came in and did a good job, as far as I was concerned I could not have enough good centre backs. The way the bookings went at the start of the season there was always the chance of losing players for a few games through suspension, so I was still looking for someone to complement the group. Eventually, I made a move for Nottingham Forest defender, Carl Tiler.

I always had an admiration for Carl, even though he had experienced a few injury problems. But he had played all last pre-season and all the way up to October without any difficulty and had re-established himself at Forest. So, at £750,000, I believed he would be a very good investment. He was that left-sided, centre-back I had been looking for at the time my attention was diverted by Mark Draper's availability.

Unfortunately for Carl, in his first game for us he ruptured a nerve in his leg, as we have since discovered. At the time no one was quite sure what it was and we anticipated he would return fairly quickly. But the injury proved to be a lot worse than was first thought, with Carl having to patiently wait for the nerve to grow back to its full length.

My other two deals during last season involved Graham Fenton, who moved to Blackburn, and Julian Joachim, who I signed from Leicester. It is always difficult for lads like Graham and Julian. In both instances I could see that if they stayed with the clubs they had grown up with they might find it difficult to become regular first team players. In Graham's case he joined Villa as a youngster, and although he broke into the senior side, he was always likely to be in for one match and out the next.

Graham was a good player – and still is – as Newcastle found to their cost towards the end of last season. I knew he would always be in my 14 or 15, but by the same token I knew he would be the one I left out if Ian Taylor or Tommy Johnson was fit. I understood he would soon become frustrated by that. So I felt Graham needed a new challenge to try to establish himself as a first team regular elsewhere, and I thought it was in his best interests to move to Ewood Park. Although he was still trying to hold down a regular first team spot as last season drew to a close, the incentive was there for him, and I am sure he will do well in the future.

Similarly, I could look over in the direction of Leicester and see young Joachim having the same sort of problems trying to establish himself. He had come trough the ranks at Filbert Street, played at England under-21 level, just like Graham, but then found his career coming to a bit of a halt after losing his way a bit. So while I believed the move to Blackburn would help Graham, by the same token I felt that Julian's career would benefit by joining us.

Hopefully, during the next few seasons my judgement will be proved right, with both youngsters going on to big things at their respective clubs. And if they do make it, then I am sure both Blackburn and ourselves will feel that we had a bargain.

The chairman's figures will always be different to mine, but in actual transfer terms up to the end of last season, I had spent £16.1m bringing new players to Villa Park while, at the same time, recouping £.9.3m in sales, if you include the John Fashanu insurance pay-out. It was certainly a bit different to the £40,000 I had to spend at Darlington all those years ago.

Chapter Eight

The Wembley Way

The League Cup, now known as the Coca-Cola Cup, is a competition that has always been a bit special to me. Stretching back over more than 25 years it has provided some very fond memories. I remember signing my first professional contract at Villa just a few days before they played against Spurs in the 1971 Final at Wembley.

I was only 17 and a few months old, when I was called into the office of manager Vic Crowe and offered a contract. That was quite a surprise to me, because in those days it was normal to serve a three-year apprenticeship before becoming a full professional, yet I had been at the club less than two seasons when I was given a pro deal.

The fact that I had been offered the contract was fantastic as far as I was concerned. We were a Third Division team at the time but it was a tremendous experience to go to Wembley to watch the Final in my new capacity, even though we lost the match. Martin Chivers, one of the country's first £100,000 signings, scored for Spurs in the 2-0 victory. Despite losing, the club held a function in London afterwards and I can remember feeling very proud as I found myself rubbing shoulders with the senior professionals for the first time.

Villa reached Wembley by beating Manchester United in the semi-finals and after that victory, while I was still an apprentice, I remember Pat McMahon giving me a £5 tip for keeping his boots clean. It was a lot of money in those days, especially when you consider I was earning only £7 a week in wages. That was the era of players like Chico Hamilton, Fred Turnbull, Ray Graydon, Andy Lochhead, as well as Bruce Rioch and Pat McMahon, the two players whose boots I had to keep clean.

By the time Villa returned to Wembley for the 1975 Final against Norwich I was fortunate enough to be a first team regular, and we won the cup that season thanks to a goal from Ray Graydon. We also stayed in London after that match and had a great celebration party. That was the season Villa gained promotion back up to the old First Division and I received my first England call-up, so lots of nice things in my life seemed to go hand in hand with this particular competition.

We were back at Wembley two years later to play Everton in the Final. That was also a very memorable season for me in as much that Andy Gray, John Deehan and I scored more than 70 goals between us. I got 26, which was as good a goalscoring season as I ever had. The only disappointment was the fact that I was unable to break back into the England set-up. I had been out for a while due to injury and by the time I was fit again the likes of Trevor Francis and Tony Woodcock had established themselves at international level, leaving no place for me.

There were replays in the League Cup Finals in those days, and after a draw at Wembley we met again at Hillsborough in a much more entertaining game than the first. But we drew again, which meant a third meeting, this time at Old Trafford. That was the match when Chris Nichol scored the goal that is still talked about to this day. I also scored twice to help secure the victory.

That 1977 team was a good one and many felt if it had stayed together a bit longer we might have won more trophies. Looking back it is difficult to criticise Ron Saunders too much for breaking it up, for within four seasons he had guided Villa to the League title. But that 1977 side was a good one to play in. We produced some exciting stuff, and that was the season we beat Liverpool 5-1 at home in a League match.

So those were my first three experiences of the League Cup, watching as a young pro and then taking part in two victories. By the time Villa reached the Final again in 1994, I was manager at Leicester City.

In October, 1993 I attended a sports writers' dinner in Manchester and won a draw prize of two tickets for the Final the following March, even though no one had any idea who would be taking part. It could even have been my own club at the time, Leicester. The joke at the time was that I would probably prefer a couple of tickets for the play-offs because Leicester had reached the play-off final in the previous two seasons and, subsequently, got there again.

As it turned out, Villa and Manchester United reached Wembley in the Coca-Cola Cup, so I took up the offer of the tickets and took along my son, Andrew, who often switched his allegiance from Leicester to United if his dad was having a bad time at Filbert Street. So it was ironic that we were travelling down to watch Villa play at Wembley, with me hoping for a Villa victory and Andrew sitting alongside me wearing a United scarf. I have to say, that a couple of years on, there is no sign of a United poster in his bedroom. He has switched to Villa, and rightly so.

I remember Villa's victory over United very well. I thought, tactically, they were fantastic and deserved the victory, even though not too many people expected them to win and subsequently deny United the treble of League title, FA Cup and Coca-Cola Cup. You may recall that my second game in charge of Villa was the match at Crystal Palace in the defence of the Coca-Cola Cup. We were well beaten, and I suppose that was the only time that my affection for the competition really went out of the window. That proved to be a bad night, to say the least.

But last season things again changed for the better. We began our League programme quite brightly, winning a few matches, and I could sense a feeling within the camp that we could genuinely do well in a cup competition. We were pleased with the early progress and were not giving much away at the back. We had a strong midfield, whichever combination we played, and Dwight and Savo were causing teams quite a few problems. So we thought we had a good cup team in the making and quite early on set our sights on getting to Wembley.

Our first Coca-Cola Cup game was Peterborough at home and, in all fairness, we could have scored any number of goals that night.

Savo was away on international duty, so Tommy came into the side and was so keen to do well, having found himself on the bench for the first few games of the season. He and Dwight caused all sorts of problems and we created loads of chances. Even though we were playing a side from the lower divisions there were signs for me during that 6-0 victory that we could have a good run in the competition. One or two Premiership sides had struggled to overcome similar opposition, yet we had dominated our first leg tie and knocked in six without reply.

I remember one or two players mentioning in the dressing room afterwards that we could do really well in the cup. Admittedly, we did not have the best of nights in the return leg at Peterborough. It was difficult to really get into the swing of things with a six-goal lead, and if ever there was an occasion last season when we cruised through a game, I suppose that was it. Even when Peterborough pulled a goal back we knew we were not in any real danger, and eventually Steve Staunton scored an equaliser.

We then drew Stockport County at home, another game we were expected to win, but still had to overcome a tricky little hurdle. I thought it was a decent game of football, with Stockport playing their part. But we scored goals at the right time, kept a clean sheet, and we were progressing very nicely. It was after we drew Queens Park Rangers at home and won 1-0 that the belief we were really going to do something in the competition grew stronger.

From then on it seemed it did not really matter who we came up against. There was the genuine feeling that it could be our season as far as the Coca-Cola Cup was concerned. Although we beat QPR by only 1-0, it could have three or four. Even though we had only a one-goal lead, we were never under any real pressure, and kept our composure.

I always maintain that it is a good sign if you can win a game 1-0 in the manner we displayed on that occasion. Once Andy Townsend put us ahead they never really threatened an equaliser.

We are not particularly noisy in the dressing room but there was a real air of confidence. Players were really up for it in their own particular way. I have noticed that when we get too loud sometimes it produces the wrong type of atmosphere. But whenever cup games came around there was this feeling that everyone was totally focused on winning.

We had players in the team with the experience to carry us through, coupled with others who were hungry for success. People like Nigel Spink, Andy Townsend, Paul McGrath and Steve Staunton had seen and done it all before. But there were also players like Dwight Yorke and Ugo Ehiogu who had missed out on Villa's Wembley success two years earlier.

Then there was Gary Charles who, a couple of years ago, had lost at Wembley with Nottingham Forest and then left the club under a bit of a cloud; Alan Wright, who during his last few months at Blackburn had been a reserve player; Tommy Johnson, who had been relegated the season before with Leicester; Gareth Southgate, who had suffered a similar fate at Crystal Palace; Ian Taylor, a staunch Villa fan who had seen his dream move come true; Savo Milosevic, who at last had the stage in English football he wanted, and maybe felt he had a point to prove. Indeed, a group of players who had a lot to prove to themselves.

That hunger and desire to do well shone through in every cup game we played. There was a period leading up to the quarter-final with Wolves when it was uncertain whether Dwight would be available. He was wanted by Trinidad and Tobago to play in the CONCACAF Cup competition in the United States, and there was a big worry for a while that he would have to miss out on the tie. Fortunately we reached agreement with the Trinidad authorities, which allowed him to remain here for the clash with Wolves before flying off to the States.

But even before he had received permission to stay with us, Dwight was talking to me privately about how much the game against Wolves meant to him.

Our next game was against Manchester United in the Premiership, which was arguably just as important. But Dwight was adamant that he was not going to miss out on the tie at Molineux because victory would put us through to the semi-finals, and he possibly feared that once he was out of the team he may not get back in. He also told me that if he missed the game and it did not go our way then he would never be able to forgive himself.

So even at that stage, before we had played in the quarter-finals, Dwight and I were talking about the prospect of reaching the Final, and even winning at Wembley to secure a place in Europe. That was how strong the feelings were between the manager and a player that this competition was growing in importance to us and was possibly there for the taking. That is why I was prepared to sacrifice Dwight for the Premiership match against United if it meant having him available to face Wolves.

Dwight's performance against Wolves was terrific. They were really up for it and made it very difficult for us. But we always had the edge and got through, thanks to a goal from Tommy Johnson. I have watched the goal time and again, and it still seems to me that Tommy actually mis-hit the shot. But sometimes they are the best, because if you strike the ball cleanly it invariably ends up straight in the keeper's arms. The goal was created by a run down the right and cross from Gary Charles, who made so many goals for us in a similar manner during the second half of the season.

Wolves put us under a bit of pressure in the last five minutes or so, but again we had the ability to hold on to a one-goal advantage to take us through to the semi-finals. We were joined in the last four by Arsenal, Leeds and neighbours, Birmingham City. With no disrespect to either Leeds or Blues, the one team we were hoping to avoid was Arsenal. Secretly, we were hoping and praying that the draw would be kind to us in that respect. I know Arsenal manager Bruce Rioch very well, of course. Remember, I cleaned his boots when I was an apprentice at Villa, and I later worked under him at Middlesbrough. So, deep down, I wanted to steer clear of Arsenal because I felt they presented us with the most difficult route to Wembley.

Inevitably, we drew Arsenal, but rather than adopt a negative approach we began saying to ourselves that if we could get past them we would WIN the Cup. That was no disrespect to either Leeds or Blues, it was just this genuine belief and positive mentality.

During my managerial career I have been involved in hundreds of matches but I can never remember another quite like the semi-final first leg at Highbury. We went into the tie very relaxed and confident, yet within what seemed no time at all we were two goals down. It does not matter who you are, you will rarely come up against a much bigger test than trying to pull back a two-goal deficit against a team like Arsenal at Highbury. After we had gone 2-0 down there was a period for about 10 minutes when I feared, for the first and only time that season, that we could actually miss out on winning the Coca-Cola Cup, and that was quite frightening.

But Dwight scored a couple of minutes before half time to get us back into it, and when I got into the dressing room at the break I just knew that my players were going to get something out of the game. The team had grown up. They were able to show tremendous battling qualities, coupled with the mentality to handle such pressures. That 15-minute break at Highbury showed me a lot about the team I had built. It was almost an eerie atmosphere, fairly quiet, but with the players looking at one another and coming out with the occasional sentence that made me realise they meant business.

Allan, John and I did not have to sit them down and lecture them on the importance of victory. They already knew that, so we went through the routine of a few reminders. Not many teams go two-down at Highbury and come away with anything, but I sensed my lads were ready to show it was possible. Sure enough, Dwight scored another great goal during the second half to tie it up at 2-2, and the mood in the dressing room afterwards suggested this was the result that would take us to Wembley.

We knew we still faced a difficult second leg at Villa Park, but we felt we had done everything in that first leg that we needed to do. Most people at Highbury agreed that we were the better side on the night, and that gave us an awful lot of confidence. But going into the second leg was still a new experience for me. I had to decide whether to pick a side I felt would go on and win the tie, overall, or one that could hold on to ensure we got through on the away goals rule.

Credit to Arsenal, they came to Villa Park and had a go at us. They were quite adventurous and, as a result, it was a fairly open game. Again, I thought we just edged it, but at the end of 90 minutes it was still goalless, which meant we went into extra time with Arsenal knowing they had absolutely nothing to lose, while we had every-thing to lose in that final half hour. But I maintain that period of extra time was as outstanding as anything we achieved throughout the whole of last season.

In effect we were protecting a one-goal advantage, because if Arsenal scored we would be out of the competition. In those circum-stances you expect players to be nervous. But in that half hour Arsenal, for all their experience, never had a sniff at goal. We kept possession, were by far the more adventurous team, and there was absolutely so sign of nerves. I maintain to this day that our performance during that vital period was as good an exhibition of cup football as anyone could wish to see.

It was during the second leg that a few eyebrows were raised when I substituted Steve Staunton, a Republic of Ireland international of vast experience, for young Riccardo Scimeca who had played only a handful of senior games at the time. Maybe a few people looked at me that night and wondered why I had made the switch. I know that sometimes when I watch matches and a manager makes a substitu-tion, I quietly question his judgement because I am looking at it in a completely different light.

Against Arsenal in the second leg I just felt the whole balance of the team was not quite right. Steve and Andy Townsend were both operating on the left side of midfield and I needed to do something to balance it up down the right. Actually, Steve was playing quite well, but the fact that I took him off appeared to be forgotten afterwards because we had won, so no one really questioned my actions. If it had gone the other way then I am sure the substitution would have been one of the first questions fired at me by the Press.

When the final whistle sounded at the end of extra time, there was just a feeling of huge relief that we had reached Wembley in my first full season in charge. I have a photograph of me punching the air in delight. It is similar to the one taken when we avoided relegation on the last day of the previous season at Norwich, only this time there was even more to celebrate. In fairness to Bruce Rioch, he came straight over to me at the end of the match, shook my hand, and told me to go to Wembley and win it.

We still did not know who we would be playing at Wembley. Leeds went to St Andrew's in the first leg of their semi-final and secured a lead in a game I watched. While Blues played well and battled hard, Leeds were always going to be favourites. They went on to win the second leg as well which meant we would be playing at Wembley against a team we lost to at Elland Road early in the season, but beat 3-0 at Villa Park only a few weeks before the Final. The only reason we lost 2-0 to Leeds at their place was because we went there believing we could not beat them. Many people suggested they were going to win the title last season.

So although there was not too much wrong with the way we played, we seemed to accept defeat as inevitable. Afterwards we had a very good conversation in the dressing room. I simply pointed out that if they wanted to win things in football they had to start believing that they could go to the likes of Elland Road, Anfield, Highbury, St James' Park and Goodison and get something out of games.

The defeat at Elland Road so early in the season was a very big lesson for all of us and it was something we took on board, not just for the League match back at Villa Park, but also in the build-up to the Final.

In the weeks leading up to Wembley lots of people were ready to offer advice, some of which I was very prepared to listen to. I suppose there are a dozen or so people in the game who speak to me regularly on the telephone. I shall not mention names because I believe it is a very private matter but, suffice to say, I value their opinions very highly. Some are my former coaches, some are managers or assistant managers, while others are no longer directly involved in the game. But as the Final got nearer they all rang me and reminded me that going to Wembley was not just a day out. They told me to go there and make sure we won. They reminded me that going to Wembley and ending up losers was a horrible experience.

So everything in the build-up to the Final was focused on going there to win a game of football. The feeling in the camp was that if we were right on the day, then nothing would stop us.

Even so, we were involved in a bit of controversy leading up to Wembley when it was suggested from some quarters that we were trying to deliberately pick up bookings so that some of our players, already close to suspension, would be able to serve any ban before the Final.

Now, believe me, if any player can plan how to get a booking these days then they are a lot more cunning than me. During February we had players like Andy Townsend, Ugo Ehiogu, Tommy Johnson and Savo Milosevic all quite close to suspension. At the same time we were not only thinking about the Coca-Cola Cup Final but were also still heavily involved in the FA Cup and important Premiership matches. My belief is that bookings should relate to the competition in which they were picked up. I feel it is wrong that, for example, a central defender could go up to ten matches without having a booking and then find himself missing a Wembley final after being cautioned in a Premiership game.

There is also a general consensus within the game that defenders who go seven or so matches without being cautioned should then have one of their bookings wiped off. These are things I am sure will be looked at more closely in future. But, as I have said, a number of our lads were facing the threat of missing Wembley. However, there was no way any of them picked up bookings on purpose, just to make sure they would serve a suspension beforehand and be ready for the big day.

Admittedly, Savo and Ugo both got booked very late in the game at Anfield and were banned just before the Final. But at the time they did not know how our fixtures would unwind, and whether or not they had actually ruled themselves out of a Wembley appearance. I dare bet hardly any player in the modern game could tell you much beyond the next game who they are due to play. They do not look that far ahead and study fixtures as supporters probably do.

Looking back, it was something that had been built up in the Press and, I have to say, was a ludicrous suggestion. In a way, I suppose, I helped bring it on myself by answering a question at a Press conference rather flippantly.

Someone said that a booking one of my players had received was only a 'two-pointer' and would, therefore, not be suspended. I sarcastically replied that it was a surprise to me because I was sure it was a 'four-pointer'. My comments were misconstrued as suggesting I was disappointed a suspension had not been reached. I have learned the lesson. I shall stop and think before I answer questions in Press conferences in a flippant manner from now on.

Leading up to the Wembley Final I had the first opportunity in two or three months to pick the side that began the season so well for me by beating Manchester United at home. So as the Final drew nearer the guessing game began as to who would be playing, but in fact it was a very simple decision for me. It is amazing that when a Cup Final draws near you can guarantee every member of your squad will be fit and available. The treatment room becomes deserted.

But I just turned the clock back to the team I had selected at the start of the season and who never really got the praise for beating United so comprehensively. That game was not about Villa in the eyes of the Press, it was all about what had gone wrong with United. Obviously, not a lot when you consider that nine months or so later they ended up as Premiership Champions.

When I made it known to the lads who would be playing at Wembley, I could again feel that air of determination, a strong belief that nothing and no one was going to stand in their way. A couple of days before the Final we travelled down to our team hotel at Selsdon Park which, as some of you may know, is right on the south side of the Capital, quite a distance from Wembley.

A lot of people may have looked at our venue and thought it was too far away to stay. But we had looked at the preparations carefully and, knowing the match was to take place on a Sunday with a five o'clock kick-off, we did not feel there was a problem. Selsdon Park is a superb hotel, very peaceful and quiet, and right on a golf course. We were very well looked after when it came to food and other facilities, while our shirt sponsors AST set up a computer games room so the players could bide away their time and relax.

During the two days at the hotel everyone conducted himself in a thoroughly professional manner. No one wanted to stay up later than was wise; everybody ate the right food; no one stepped out of line for an instant. There was never a thought in my head that I would have to pull someone aside and remind them not to do certain things. They were there knowing there was a job to be done, and they were ready for it.

So I felt those two days of preparation were spot on. I was quoted afterwards as saying that even the traffic lights changed to green for us on the journey from the hotel to Wembley. It was not quite that simple, although I have to say our police motorcycle outrider did a magnificent job. He did everything to ensure we had a smooth run, and when we actually got to Wembley he was so pleased with himself he sat there with a beaming smile on his face.

Even he admitted he did not think the trip would run quite so smoothly. But he was King of the Road for close to an hour and I think he enjoyed himself that day almost as much as we did. Even the lads enjoyed the trip to Wembley watching this guy operate. I have to say he was unbelievable and helped make our day perfect.

As we walked out at Wembley to take on Leeds I knew I had a group of players who had prepared themselves thoroughly for what was ahead. They had done everything I asked of them. They were not the sort who had heard the bell go and just come running out. Perhaps Brian Little did a few times in his playing career, but not these lads. I had not talked too much about the opposition during the days leading up to the match. I very rarely do.

It is all right saying you have to be careful of such and such, or that a certain player may cause us problems, and then on the day of the match you find out the person you have been talking about is not even playing. We have a plan of how we want to play and we concentrate on that. I knew how I wanted us to play against Leeds, using our three central defenders and two wing-backs in front of a goalkeeper who is as good as anyone in the country. Then there is a midfield trio who complement one another. Townsend, who leads by example and wants to be everywhere, Taylor who works his socks off winning the ball and very rarely wasting it, and Draper who is capable of winning any game for you.

Finally, there are the two lads up front, who can score goals and will only get better. I always said leading up to Wembley that Savo would probably score our most important goal of the season. As it happened his goal in the Final proved to be just that. I am sure our supporters will remember his tremendous shot for many years to come. It set us on our way to a memorable and comfortable victory. All we had to do was make sure we did not freeze on the day – and we didn't. There were about eight minutes remaining and we were heading for success when, I admit, that I upset Tommy Johnson. You may remember he had recovered from injury only just before the Final, so had to content himself with a place on the substitutes' bench.

Tommy was desperate to get into the action. After warming up and stretching for a few minutes he turned to me and asked to be put on for the remaining few minutes. I must have given him one of those looks that said everything, because it seemed to knock the stuffing out of him, and he just sat down and watched the rest of the game. We have often talked about it since and I have reassured him no malice was intended. It was just a case of me being totally focused on the game and I had put up the 'Do Not Disturb' sign.

After the final whistle had sounded and Andy and the lads went up to receive the cup, I just looked around to soak up some of the atmosphere and then made my way to the dressing room. To be perfectly honest, I was shattered and just wanted to go and a sit down. As I have already said I am not the type to be jumping around, I let the young lads do things like that.

It was only afterwards that I realised the Villa supporters had been shouting for me to come back out on to the pitch. If I had known I would have been only too happy to do so. Some people thought it was because I was too shy, but I can assure everyone that was not the reason. As it happened, I was back down the tunnel giving radio and television interviews long before the players came in.

But I can say without any fear of contradiction that every one of my players was able to come off the Wembley pitch at the end, sit in the dressing room and know he played well. Often you can win games and one or two players know they have not been at their best, so they tend to sit there a bit subdued at the end. But this was one occasion when every one of them was able to hold his head high, knowing the platform had been built and it was up to them to go on and win more honours in the future.

Chapter Nine

So Near, Yet So Far

Although I have a strong affection for the League Cup, unfortunately the same cannot be said for the other major domestic knockout competition, and arguably the most glamourous of them all, the FA Cup.

My first memory of the FA Cup was scoring a cracking goal against Manchester United when I was a young player at Villa, back in the 1976-77 season. We were playing at Old Trafford and I beat Alex Stepney with a shot from about 30 yards. But we still lost that game 2-1, so perhaps I should have known then that it was never going to be the kindest of competitions for me.

The furthest I ever reached as a player was when we got to the quarter-finals three years later before losing to West Ham. That proved to be one of my last full games for Villa before my career was ended by a knee injury. I remember one or two of our more experienced players were suspended for that game, including Allan Evans and Kenny Swain. So we had several youngsters in the line-up. Brendan Ormsby, Ivor Linton and Terry Bullivant all played, if my memory serves me correct.

The match had moved into injury time and it was still goalless. We were looking forward to taking West Ham back to Villa Park for a replay when they were awarded a penalty. The ball came over from a corner and Ken McNaught supposedly handled. Yes, the hand did touch the ball, but whether it was deliberate is open to debate. The referee decided, however, that it was a penalty, and Ray Stewart blasted in the spot kick to knock us out. Incidentally, West ham went on to win the cup that season as a then Second Division side, beating Arsenal 1-0, thanks to a rare headed goal from Trevor Brooking.

If we had held on for a draw we would have met West Ham in a replay at Villa Park the following Wednesday. But because we had been beaten we played a re-arranged League game at home to Wolves on the Monday night, and it was during that game that I suffered the knee injury which subsequently forced me to quit.

I have often thought about the sequence of events since. Perhaps if West Ham had not been awarded their last-gasp penalty we would have been playing them instead of Wolves, I would not have been injured and, maybe, could have continued playing until I was 35 instead of 27. I know it is all ifs and maybes, but in my quieter moments the thought has often crossed my mind.

Last season it was not until we reached the semi-finals that it really hit me that it was the furthest Villa had progressed in the cup since reaching the last four a full 36 years earlier, when they lost 1-0 to Wolves at The Hawthorns. I do not think it really dawned on any of us just how far away this club had been from the competition until we started reading in the Press that we were in the semis for the first time since 1960, and trying to win it for the first time since 1957.

I suppose the first few games in the FA Cup last season were fairly low key, so it was not until we drew Liverpool in the last four that cup fever really began to take a hold. Our third round tie was away to non-League, Gravesend and Northfleet. Thankfully they switched the game to Villa Park. In fairness, while I still think we would have won at their place, I am sure it would have been a lot more difficult in many respects. It was one of those matches that we knew we would receive little praise for, whether we won 1-0 or 10-0.

So before a ball was kicked we emphasised to the players that the most important thing was just to win the game and ignore what might be said afterwards. We reminded them to treat the opposition with respect, even though they were a non-League team, and to treat the tie in a professional manner. Fortunately, we scored an early goal to settle any nerves, and although the opposition had nothing to lose, and had a real go at us, we eventually emerged 3-0 winners. In a way, it was an occasion when everyone ended up winners. Gravesend and Northfleet players, officials and supporters all seemed to enjoy themselves, and good relationships were forged between the two clubs to such a degree that we willingly agreed to send a young side down there recently to play a pre-season friendly fixture.

Having spent some time in non-League myself, I realise how important these type of relationships can be. I maintain that you should never feel that high and mighty as to only look down from afar on such clubs.

They willingly agreed to let us use the home dressing room at Villa Park for the third round tie, even though we played in the away kit. I spoke to their manager by phone before the game, asking if they had any particular requests, and he was very nice about the whole thing. They did not try to pull any tricks to upset us and we sensed all along that they were just happy to draw us in the cup, determined to make the most of it. We did not read any reports of the match afterwards, just to make sure there were no seeds of doubt planted in our minds because we had scored only three goals against a non-League team. I know we would have needed to reach double figures for people to say that we underlined the difference between Premiership football and non-League, but overall we were quite satisfied with the day's work.

Our next game in the competition took us to Sheffield United for a fourth round tie, and in the week leading up to the match very few people thought it would actually take place on schedule. Most of the country was covered in deep snow, and although our tie had been put back 24 hours to the Sunday so it could be televised live, when we drove up to Sheffield on the Saturday we could not believe for one minute that the game would even have half a chance of taking place.

We even struggled to reach the team hotel which was only a few minutes away from Bramall Lane. The coach had to go up a hill to reach the hotel, and halfway up there was a set of traffic lights. Our coach driver, Mick, kept saying to me that if the lights changed to red and we had to stop, then we would probably end up sliding right back down to the bottom of the hill. That is how bad the conditions were.

As we got nearer to the lights, even the players started joining in the banter, shouting: "Go on, Mick, you can do it." It was touch and go, but thankfully the lights did remain on green and we just made it. When we arrived at the hotel we discovered that a coach load of people on their way to Bournemouth had been stranded there for two days because of the Arctic conditions. So it was an achievement in itself just to have travelled from Birmingham to Sheffield.

But it was one of those days that, as a manager, you are worried. I sensed the players did not think the game would take place. They were beginning to switch off rather than concentrate their thoughts on trying to reach the next round. So Allan, John and I worked over-time instilling into them the fact that there was just a chance it could go ahead and made sure they were preparing themselves properly. Ironically, we discovered afterwards that one or two Sheffield players got into a bit of trouble because they had gone out the night before the game, thinking it would not be on.

The following morning conditions had not really improved but John and I got up fairly early and managed to struggle down to Bramall Lane to look at the pitch. When we arrived we could hardly believe what we saw. There were literally hundreds of people with spades and shovels, clearing the snow off the pitch, terraces and even the car parks. We could see straight away that the match would take place that afternoon after all.

We went straight back to the hotel and told the lads the game would be on. More often than not our routine on the morning of a match is to go for a walk rather than do any real training. It gives everyone a chance to stretch their limbs and for us to have a chat about the game. So we all set off from the hotel in thick snow for our loosener. Not surprisingly, there were a few snowballs flying around our ears before too long. But it was still difficult to imagine the game would take place because of the conditions we found ourselves in, and the fact that the majority of matches the previous day had been postponed because of the weather.

But Sheffield had worked their socks off and the game was able to go ahead. Potentially, it was very difficult for us and it was made no easier by the fact that a certain Gordon Cowans had recently joined them. Howard Kendall had become their new manager and although they were still in the bottom three of the First Division, the improvements had begun to take place. I kept thinking to myself that of all the people who could ruin a good cup run for us, please don't let it be Sid Cowans, a player I knew very well, had played alongside, and who had been a tremendous servant to Villa in three separate spells.

We played very well for the first 20 minutes but, again, did not get a goal, which was a bit of a worry to us. Remember, in the previous round Sheffield had knocked out Arsenal. Allan and I watched that game and, in fairness, they deserved the victory. Really, they should have won by more than one goal. Fortunately, they did not produce the same type of performance against us and eventually we sneaked through with a goal that I am sure will be remembered and shown on television for many years to come.

Alan Wright volleyed a ball out to Tommy Johnson who knocked it into the box for Savo Milosevic. Savo was brought down for a penalty, with half of Sheffield claiming that he had taken a dive. That is the sort of thing you do get these days. Every time a visiting striker goes down in the area, the home fans are calling for him to be booked for diving. Naturally, it puts the referee under pressure, but on this occasion he judged that Savo had been brought down and awarded the spot kick. Looking back, it was probably the right decision.

Dwight Yorke stepped up to take the penalty and the rest is history. Dwight had already told a few of his team mates that the next time he took a spot kick he was just going to chip the keeper, rather than place the ball into one of the corners. And when you consider he took the kick against Alan Kelly, an international goalkeeper of vast experience, it makes the incident even more incredible. I have seen players in the past chip the ball into a corner. I recall Gary Lineker scoring and missing in that way. But Dwight just knocked the ball straight towards the keeper, gambling that he would move one way or the other.

He also did it in an FA Cup tie when the scores were still level and the match was being screened live on television. Some people look on Dwight as a quiet guy but, after that penalty, so much for shy Dwight! Even when I watch the goal on television now, for a second or two it is still difficult to see what is actually going on. It looks as though he has chipped the ball over the bar. I remember Steve Staunton, one of our substitutes that day, looking at me and laughing because I think my jaw had dropped so much in disbelief it had almost hit the ground.

People have often asked me what I said to Dwight afterwards. I simply said, brilliant. Of course I would probably have had more to say if it had not gone in and have told Dwight he must learn from the mistake. But there was no need for that. In a way this was a first, and I am sure we shall see other players try it in future. But it is more likely to be when their team is four goals up in the last minute, rather than at 0-0 in such an important cup tie. As cheeky as it was, it proved to be our winner, and that earned us a trip to Ipswich in the fifth round.

This was another potentially hazardous tie because some people may have forgotten that Ipswich had just knocked out Blackburn. I can now reveal for the first time that once more there were problems leading up to the match. This time it was not snow, but food that was our big cause for concern. As usual, we travelled down to an hotel for an overnight stay but, unfortunately, things were not as we would have hoped.

When our evening meal was brought in it could only be described as poor, and very few of the lads ate any of it. Footballers are very particular about what they eat and once something like that happens, then you can guarantee that, in their minds, everything else was going to be wrong as well. That meant the beds were uncomfortable, and breakfast was not right either. My staff were trying to keep minds trained on the match but it was hardly the best preparation for a fifth round tie.

We were concerned that things were not right and I know that if anything had gone wrong early on then everyone had the excuses tucked in their back pockets that they had either not eaten properly or slept well. If Ipswich had known about our problems then they would possibly have tried to take the game by the scruff of the neck and try to ruffle us even more. As it happened, they actually sat back and let us dictate the early proceedings.

Their tactics appeared to be that they were happy to keep the score at 0-0 with the hope that they might sneak a goal late on. That suited us fine and we were soon two goals ahead through Mark Draper and Dwight Yorke. From then on we never looked back. Ian Taylor came on as substitute and scored the third in a decisive 3-1 victory.

The reward for that victory was the fact that we went straight from Portman Road to the nearest McDonald's Restaurant to give everyone something to eat. Normally, we have sandwiches on the coach for the journey home. The sandwiches were there on this occasion, but they had come from the hotel we had stayed at. Naturally, the lads were not interested in them, So, after the problems we had encountered, yet still won, we decided for once to give them a treat. This was their first food for about a day and a half, and they had earned it.

The next round took us to Nottingham Forest. Although we played Gravesend and Northfleet at Villa Park, technically it was an away match, so our trip to the City Ground was our fourth successive away tie. Yet people were finally thinking that we might do something in the competition, perhaps reach the semi-finals for the first time in 36 years. We had already drawn twice with Forest in the Premiership and, in my opinion, had played better than them on each occasion.

I knew we had a chance of victory, even though we were without Tommy Johnson through injury and Andy Townsend because of suspension. I had signed Franz Carr in the deal that saw Garry Parker move to Leicester although, because of the system we played, Franz's first team chances had been very limited. However, sometimes a manager has a gut feeling about something and my feeling for the sixth round tie with Forest was that Franz should be given a chance in Tommy's role.

He had done well in the reserves and battled hard to try to establish himself as a regular first team player, without too much success, simply because he was a winger and we were playing without an out-and-out wide man. But against Forest I thought to myself that if ever there was a day for a player to come up trumps for us against his former club, this was it. So I played my hunch.

As it turned out Franz played very well, and scored a great goal that proved to be the winner. He ribbed me a bit afterwards that he should have been given more chances, but when you are a manager you cannot afford to let sentiment come into your thinking. Although I felt we should have beaten Forest by a bigger margin, Franz's goal proved enough to put us through to the semi-finals where we were joined by Liverpool, Manchester United and Chelsea.

When I looked at the teams still in the competition, I knew that if any was going to give us a hard time it would probably be Liverpool. Even though Manchester United went on to win the double, at the time, we had played against them twice and had not lost. Although we lost to Chelsea at home in the Premiership, we were a better team than them, so in reality the side we really wanted to avoid were Liverpool. That did not happen. We were paired and we knew it was going to be a tough one.

However, I was pleased that I was able to put out the side that began the season for us, and we started well enough. Unfortunately, we then lost Gareth Southgate through injury,and it was while he was off the pitch, before he was forced off permanently, that Liverpool went in front. I genuinely believe there is not much between Liverpool and ourselves, but they tended to have all the little breaks against us last season and the semi-final proved no different. In the end the scoreline did not do us justice, but the fact remained that our hopes of reaching Wembley for the second time in the season had been ended at Old Trafford.

Looking back I have to say it was a strange week for us. The previous Sunday we beat Leeds in the Coca-Cola Cup. Immediately after that victory and celebration party that followed, the likes of Mark Bosnich, Savo Milosevic, Ugo Ehiogu, Gareth Southgate, Paul McGrath, Steve Staunton and Paul McGrath going off to play in international matches for their respective countries. They did not return until the following Friday, just 48 hours before our semi-final with Liverpool.

To this day I am not making excuses for our defeat, Liverpool also had players away on international duty. But perhaps the difference was that our lads were still on a high after our Wembley success, and it was not until the following Friday that my staff and I had the opportunity to bring them back down to earth and concentrate their minds on the Liverpool game. Don't get me wrong, if the same thing were to happen again this season I would settle for it because it would mean another trophy in the cabinet.

But I would have liked a bit more time to do some serious talking, which is not something I do very often. The defeat was a major disappointment. I can still see us getting on our team coach outside Old Trafford feeling pretty dejected, while Liverpool were getting on their coach feeling on top of the world. I am sure we shall learn from the experience. It is a horrible feeling to lose a semi-final and I am certain if we reach that stage again, some of my players will be determined not to experience the disappointment of defeat again.

I still have this gut feeling that we are not as far away from the Liverpool level as some people might think, even though we lost to them three times last season.

Chapter Ten

My Premiership A to Z

It has often been stated that the Premiership is the toughest league in the world to play in. I would like to go one step further by saying that, in my opinion, it is now the best league in the world. You only have to look at the standard of play, week in, week out, the quality of the players involved, and the sheer passion of the supporters.

I maintain it does not matter where you go, you would struggle to find anything better. I love the involvement, being the manager of a big club battling against the rest for the honour of becoming champions. As a season unfolds you know one thing is for certain, somewhere along the way you are going to taste defeat. But my main aim is to try to ensure those defeats are as few as possible.

I have mentioned several times already that preparation is a key word in my style of management. I never over-emphasise the strengths and weaknesses of the opposition, I just try to prepare my players properly for the job in hand. But I thought it may give everyone a better insight into the way I plan for matches if I reveal my own personal views of the teams we shall be coming up against during this season. So here is my A to Z of the Premiership, and before anyone starts thinking I do not know my alphabet, let me say I will leave this season's three newcomers, and those who were relegated in May, until last.

ARSENAL

It was widely talked about during last season that Bruce Rioch had gone to Highbury to change Arsenal's style. But while Dennis Bergkamp was signed to give a variation to their play, I still see them as fairly set in the way they operate. They still rely heavily on the defensive qualities that have held them in good stead over the years. I always regard Arsenal as a shrewd, clever team, because they are one of the few who still hold their line defensively and have the ability to catch the opposition offside.

During last season I felt the game generally was being spread out a lot more, but Arsenal still compact their play, making it extremely difficult for forwards to run through them. The likes of Tony Adams, Lee Dixon and Nigel Winterburn are clever players who try to dictate the game to forwards. They don't let them settle, they don't let them stand where they want to stand. They are always pretending to be pushing out, and then stepping back. That is something you have to contend with when you come up against Arsenal. They are very good at killing the flow of your team by constantly catching you offside. As a result you have to encourage your midfield players to get beyond their defence.

At the other end of the park, I still feel they could become a revelation by persisting with Ian Wright, Bergkamp and Paul Merson in completely free roles. When we played them in the Coca-Cola Cup semi-final last season I looked on those three as a formidable trio. Wright pushes right on to defenders, which is quite ironic, because he operates exactly the way his defenders are trying to prevent opposition forwards from playing. He turns it full circle, based on the fact that not many other teams push out as much as Arsenal. I think if Wright was actually playing against Arsenal, week in, week out, rather than for them, then he would be caught offside one hell of a lot because he pushes up so tight.

Towards the end of last season Bruce had his team playing with three centre backs, two full backs tucked in, and with those three dangerous forwards up front. I thought that was a recipe for how they might operate in future. Last season they turned the corner to a point, but many of the old habits are still there. I think if they do play three centre backs, for example, it is going to be very difficult to squeeze up and play the offside trap because the opposition will play balls down the 'channels' for players to run on to. But one thing is for sure, Arsenal will always be an awkward team to play against. They are very highly respected throughout the Premiership.

A lot was made of our achievements last season, winning the Coca-Cola Cup, semi-finalists in the FA Cup and finishing fourth in the Premiership, but it should not be overlooked that Arsenal were Coca-Cola Cup semi-finalists, and finished only one place below us in the League. There is that fine dividing line between success and failure and in his first season at Highbury Bruce was very close to a great deal of success. They qualified for Europe, and over the next few seasons I can see Arsenal figuring prominently in the chase for honours.

BLACKBURN ROVERS

Blackburn won the Premiership title the season before last on the back of their unbelievable appetite for success and their belief in being able to drag out 1-0 victories. Because of their magnificent attitude during that spell they thoroughly deserved to win the championship. But when you have achieved the success in the way they did, the opposition tend to give you a lot more respect. Suddenly, last season, Blackburn were facing sides who were inviting them to come forward and see what they could do, rather than carry the game to them.

Because they had been such a strong counter-attacking team 12 months earlier, we went to Ewood Park last season intent on not over committing ourselves and then suddenly having to chase back as they broke forward quickly on the break.

Obviously, Alan Shearer was a major threat for Blackburn before his dramatic move to Newcastle a couple of weeks before the start of the new season. You always concentrate your efforts on trying to stop him, but sometimes it does not matter how much time you spend on Alan, he will still crack one in from outside the penalty area. He has a happy knack of being able to hit the target with virtually every shot and from almost any angle.

But I felt that because Blackburn were not a real flair-type team, they found difficulty in breaking us down. They found it harder to take the initiative rather than work the opposition, and then look for the quick break. We tried to take advantage of the fact that they were strong, rather than adventurous. The fact that Kenny Dalglish stepped down probably made a difference to them because he was always going be a hard act to follow, even if you worked closely along-side him, as Ray Harford did before taking over.

However, towards the end of last season I had the impression that Ray was about to make them a real force again. He was changing the staff and bringing in the type of players capable of taking the game to the opposition, such as Lars Bohinen, a player with the ability to get forward from midfield into the opposition penalty area. Ray also brought in Chris Coleman, an excellent defender who I was linked very strongly with at the beginning of last season. But the fact that I had moved Gareth Southgate to the centre of defence meant I did not go down that road when Coleman was eventually allowed to leave Crystal Palace.

I have to say, though, that if he had been available when I was interested in him, he could well have been in my defence now, with Gareth in midfield and Mark Draper possibly not even with us. It was no surprise to me when Coleman finally moved to a big club like Blackburn and I am sure he and Colin Hendry will develop into a fine defensive partnership.

I have spoken to Ray Harford a lot in recent months. The one conclusion I have drawn is the fact that if he had been in charge when I enquired about Alan Wright we would not have been allowed to sign him. Ray is a big admirer of Alan and has often told me he was sorry to see him leave Ewood Park. But you may recall I was able to buy Alan because Kenny had brought in Graeme Le Saux, who went on to win England honours before his unfortunate injury. For me it was a case of doing a good bit of business at the right time. If I had delayed the deal any longer then Alan might still have been with Blackburn.

When you consider it is only a few years since Blackburn got into the Premiership through the play-offs, it is remarkable the progress they have made in such a short space of time.

To have won the championship so quickly was a fantastic achievement, and I am sure they will again figure prominently in the forthcoming seasons.

CHELSEA

Whenever anyone referred to Chelsea last season then it was a fair bet that Ruud Gullit also got a mention in the conversation. From a personal point of view I felt that Gullit was at his best early in the season when he was playing as a sweeper, or central defender, who had the freedom to move forward with the ball. Some people would look at Gullit and say that the nearer he is to your goal, the more problems he is going to cause.

But on the two occasions we played them last season I genuinely felt he was far more effective as a defender deeper down the park rather than he was pushing forward. Whenever they broke up attacks and he was at the back, more often than not, they just gave him the ball. I felt he created so many problems from deep. He was spraying 50 or 60-yard passes around the pitch, yet no one could call it long-ball stuff.

His passing was so accurate and deadly it was untrue, and he was able to set up so many dangerous attacks. So, for me, he was always at his best playing at the back for Chelsea. The way he and his team mates passed the ball around at the back certainly tired out my players because they found themselves chasing shadows.

Gullit had the happy knack of never being caught in possession, no matter how tight the situation was. Yet when he moved forward into midfield or attack I felt he lost his effectiveness in the hustle and bustle of the Premiership.

Overall, Chelsea were a team who got very close to honours. They reached the semi-finals of the FA Cup and it almost proved to be a great season for Glenn Hoddle before he moved on to even bigger things as successor to England coach Terry Venables. Somehow his team promised so much yet did not quite deliver. As the season wore on I am sure many teams felt they always had a chance of beating Chelsea. You know they can play – but you always have the opportunity to score goals against them. In my opinion that will always be their Achilles heel until they manage to put it right.

Gullit has now taken over as manager and, because of the experience he has picked up in different countries, I am sure his methods at Chelsea will be ones that many managers will keep a close eye on. Ruud always comes over as an enormously talented player on the pitch and a real nice guy off it. But he has had experience in Italy, for example, where it is common to train twice a day.

So behind the placid exterior I think there will be a ruthless streak, with demands on his players extremely high. He knows only too well it takes more than just talent to get to the top. He has worked very hard over the years to achieve what he has and that is one message he will be instilling into his players at Stamford Bridge.

COVENTRY CITY

The last couple of times we have visited Highfield Road we have had a great laugh. But before anyone there gets annoyed, let me emphasise it has nothing to do with the way Coventry play. It is just that when we get into the visiting dressing room we have to decide who is going to hang up Alan Wright's clothes for him. The clothes pegs are so high on the wall that you have to almost be a giant standing on tiptoe to reach them. So imagine what it is like for Alan, all 5ft 2ins of him. Even before we get to the ground we have a laugh and joke about it, and that helps to create a very relaxed dressing room whenever we play there.

For Coventry, as a team, they can be very exciting at times. We went there last season we beat them 3-0 but it could easily have been 4-4 at half time. When we watched them a couple of times early in the season we got the impression that they were just hell bent on scoring against the opposition. As a result, they can be quite vulnerable early on.

They are always pumped up and eager to get at the opposition by pushing the ball out to their wide man to hit into the penalty area. But

I found that tends to leave them a bit exposed at the back in the opening five minutes or so. Remember, Dwight Yorke scored against them after only 13 seconds in our 3-0 victory.

I always find the club's end of season video teaches you a lot about what has gone on throughout the campaign. I am sure that when Ron Atkinson watches Coventry's video he will know what I am saying. In my opinion Coventry need to be more aware of the opposition in the first five or 10 minutes of a match. You always pump up your team and make sure they are ready before a game, but a lot of teams at the top end of the table adopt the mentality of making sure they do not concede a goal in the opening 20 minutes and then take it from there.

Coventry are one of those sides you know will come at you straight away. As a result, gaps normally appear which you try to exploit. That means they can often find themselves a goal down before they have really started. I am sure they will be working very hard during the new season to make sure that does not happen any more.

They have some super individual players. On their day the likes of John Salako and Peter Ndlovu are really exciting. Noel Whelan, who joined from Leeds, surely has a great future in the game, while Dion Dublin will always weigh in with his fair share of goals.

So they have enormous potential going forward and are often as entertaining and exciting as anyone would wish to see. However, they do cause problems for themselves on a lot of occasions because, even when you are under the cosh against them, they always give you the opportunity to break away and score. That will always knock the stuffing out of a team and I guess that was their major problem last season.

EVERTON

I maintain that Everton are physically the toughest team in the Premiership to play against. They have unquestioned talent but, at the same time, Joe Royle has instilled into them a lot of the qualities they possessed when he played for them. I remember whenever I played against Everton they were a good side, brave and tough with someone like Mick Lyons always likely to come straight through you.

They worked their socks off, never let you settle, and then took advantage of that. The ordinary supporter, perhaps, does not see that in Everton's make up. But the one message I always give my players before we play them is that the first thing we must do is go out and try to match them for workrate.

They are so quick to close you down in the middle of the park that there is never any time to dwell on the ball. I remember having to tell Mark Draper last season not to bother about bringing the ball down and looking around to pass it because if he tried to do that they would be on him like a shot.

Defensively, they are also a no-risk team. Joe has taught them not to take any chances. If they find themselves under pressure they just clear their lines and start again.

All round they have quality players but, at the same time, they are not scared of hard work. For example Andrei Kanchelskis is a superb winger. He works like hell up and down the line, helping to protect his full back. Similarly, Anders Limpar worked very hard whenever he played. When Joe has his full team fit, they are a threat to anyone, particularly with someone like Duncan Ferguson leading the line. He is a young lad who has had his fair share of problems but if he can stay fully fit he is capable of taking the Premiership by storm.

The demands Joe puts on his players are quite phenomenal, probably based on some of the characters he used to play alongside at Goodison. So if any player thinks he is going to have an easy time against Everton then he is definitely kidding himself. When you come off the field having played against them you know you have been in a game of football.

I know that when Everton played at Villa Park last season Joe was very disappointed because he did not think they were as competitive as they should have been. That was his major criticism of his team that day and it is something that does not happen too often.

LEEDS UNITED

If Everton are the toughest team in the Premiership then I have to say that Elland Road is, arguably, the most intimidating ground we have to visit. My message to my players whenever we go there is just to try and get through the opening 20 minutes without conceding a goal. For although the Leeds crowd can be very partisan, urging their team to victory, they can often get a bit restless if the early goal does not arrive.

Leeds began last season as one of the hot tips to win the title and they began unbelievably well. It has been well documented that when we went there early in the campaign we did not win because we did not believe we could.

One of their big assets is the way they work at the opposition, trying to prevent you from playing. But the longer a game goes without a goal the more they become tired and their supporters become frustrated, and that gives you that little chance to get something out of the game.

It is ironic that last season Howard Wilkinson probably got as much stick as he has ever taken at Elland Road. Yet he was just that thin line away from being successful in as much that Leeds reached the Coca-Cola Cup final, only to lose to us. Howard is one of the game's great tacticians who studies the opposition and then picks his team accordingly. He often picks the same team but uses a different formation just to counter what he anticipates various teams will throw at him.

I always know that when we go to Elland Road we have probably been watched by them half a dozen times. They will have done their homework on us and, as a result, pick a team for the day. For instance, when we went up there last season big Brian Deane played on Alan Wright. They hit an unbelievable amount of high balls to him -to knock back into the middle. With Howard it almost becomes a battle of wits before the game even starts. He is very thorough, very well organised, and probably gets a lot of managers thinking about what he might be trying in any particular match.

That is where Howard and I differ enormously because we begin with a system we feel is right and if we have to adjust during a match we will. But he would probably look at my team and then say 'we will do this to counter-act them'. So I guess that is a different philosophy on the game of football from two entirely different people.

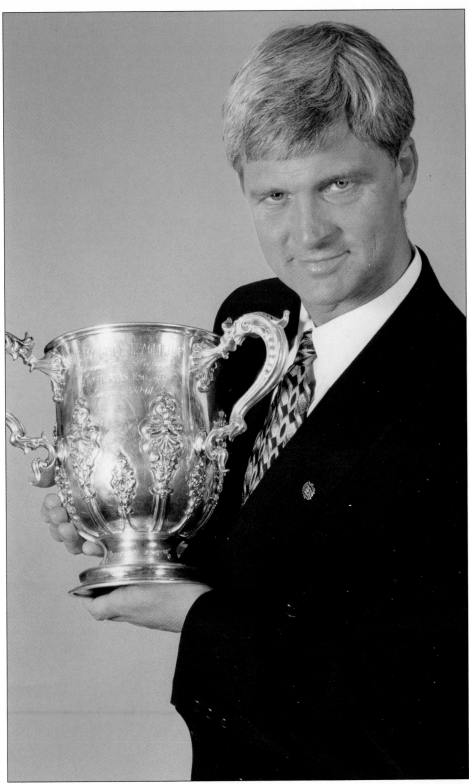

CUP OF JOY... and hopefully the first of many.

Bernard Gallagher

SITTING ON THE FENCE... but only when I am relaxing at home.

Bernard Gallagher

COUNTING MY CHICKENS... but I never put all my eggs in one basket.

Bernard Gallagher

AMONG THE ROSES... for the sweet smell of success.   Bernard Gallagher

RIDING HIGH... so the grass does not grow under my feet.   Bernard Gallagher

THE DAY I GOT THE MANAGER'S JOB... and the Chairman seems happy enough. Neville Williams

MY SUMMER SIGNING... Fernando Nelson from Sporting Lisbon. Bernard Gallagher

Bill Goulden

REMEMBER ME...? For those of you too young to recall, this was yours truly in my playing days with Aston Villa.

JUMPING FOR JOY... We have just beaten Arsenal to reach the Coca-Cola Cup Final. EMPICS

PYRAMID MANAGEMENT... Myself, Allan Evans and John Gregory.

Neville Williams

ASTON VILLA – COCA-COLA LEAGUE CUP WINNERS 1996

Bernard Gallagher

LIVERPOOL

If I had to name my *Player of the Season* for last season then, for all the brilliance of the likes of Eric Cantona and Ryan Giggs, I would have to go for Jason McAteer at Liverpool. I thought he was quite unbelievable playing as a full back, pushing on, or wing back as they are commonly known these days. When we went to Anfield and lost 3-0 I have never seen a better performance than he produced that day in that particular role.

One of the features of our play last season was Alan Wright and Gary Charles pushing forward down the flanks. But when we were beaten at Anfield I thought McAteer was absolutely outstanding, almost on another planet, although this is the first time I have publicly admitted it. As a team Liverpool play a similar game to us but are more patient. We are a mobile side who get the ball from A to B, quickly. They operate the same way but do not mind how long it takes. That is the major difference between the two teams.

Apart from Liverpool, no team playing our system beat us last season. But I have to say that on the three occasions we met them, they beat us well. Perhaps there was a period in the semi-final at Old Trafford, when they were 1-0 up, that we shaded the game. But that was about it. It is a fair bet that Liverpool will win the Premiership title again inside the next two or three seasons. You only have to look at their strength in depth.

Apart from McAteer, they have one of the best keepers in the country in David James. Then there are Stan Collymore and Robbie Fowler up front. You can look at some strikers and know that he will only shoot from outside the box, while others only come alive inside the box. But Fowler scores every type of goal there is in the book. For a little fella he scores great goals with his head. He scores from outside the box, inside it, with his left foot or right foot. He was probably the biggest thorn in our side last season. I could go on and on about Liverpool, because they have something in every department. There is not a weak link.

As far as manager Roy Evans is concerned, Liverpool undoubtedly have one of the game's nice guys at the helm. But deep down Roy is a real steely character. Whenever I have met him he has come over as a true gentleman. But I only have to look at him in the dug-out to realise just how professional and into the game he and his backroom staff are. When I played under Ron Saunders he was always on about how Liverpool did this and that, and I suppose that is what is in my system in many respects. You look at how teams are run and there is no doubt in my mind that Liverpool are spot on. Generally their players are very relaxed off the park, but they really are a determined bunch on it. So if anyone asks me who my favourite team are, other than Villa, then I would have to say Liverpool, and I believe they are going to be the ones to beat over the next few years.

MANCHESTER UNITED

When we went to Old Trafford last season and drew 1-1, we got absolutely pulverised for 45 minutes. Afterwards Alex Ferguson suggested he was disappointed that we had gone there only looking for a point. One or two Press guys tried to get me to respond at the time, no doubt hoping to build up an argument between Alex and myself. I declined, but now for the first time I will reveal that there was no way we were just looking for a draw.

In one game last season at Arsenal we went there trying to defend and came unstuck. After that I said we would never attempt it again because once we were behind we never had the mentality to get back into it. So it was not a case of putting up the shutters at Old Trafford. It was just that United were so good in the second half we could do absolutely nothing about it.

We are talking here about a team who were written off at the start of last season just because they came to our place and were well beaten. But they have some exceptional talent.

None more so than Eric Cantona. It was while we were up at Old Trafford that I saw Eric standing by the tunnel entrance. I dearly wanted to go over to him, shake him by the hand and introduce myself. In the end I decided I dare not. Let me put that statement in perspective.

Only last summer I went up to Johan Cruyff, shook his hand and introduced myself. When I was at Leicester George Best came to a function and I went up to him, shook his hand and introduced myself. We are talking there about two true footballing greats. Similarly, I wanted to meet Cantona but, in the end, didn't quite get around to it.

But what a player! You can watch him from the stand or on television, and you can see the talent. But down there near the touchline you see a different game. It is only when you are that close that you realise what an amazing talent he is. He also gives United a belief that they are going to win every time they go out on to the pitch. Alex brought a lot of youngsters into the team at the beginning of last season when the likes of Mark Hughes, Paul Ince and Andrei Kanchelskis moved on. Cantona has undoubtedly been the inspiration and driving force for many of the kids.

Of course there is outstanding talent in other departments, with Giggs the prime example. But then you put this Frenchman in amongst them and there is always the feeling that they are going to be winners. Andy Cole was given a hard time last season, but I felt he caused so many problems to so many teams. Potentially, he is a guy who could score an unbelievable amount of goals, just as he did at Newcastle.

Alex Ferguson is someone who many managers look up to, including myself. You only have to account for his achievements over the last five years. It is not easy to win the title, but to keep a team at the top, week in, week out; month in, month out; even year in, year out, is fantastic.

Everyone in the game is aware of United and what they can do. But it seems no one has come up with the answer of how to make it more difficult for them. Somehow Alex has managed to stay one jump ahead.

MIDDLESBROUGH

I worked at Middlesbrough for three years shortly after they just managed to avoid going out of existence. So to see them in the Premiership now with some of the guys I worked with still there and all in a super new stadium, is very pleasing to me. When you have worked at a club you always have an affection for it and I am delighted to see them back in the top flight. Bryan Robson has done a great job there employing tactics generally based on using three centre-backs, which he had to change occasionally because of injuries.

Whenever you play them you know they will make it hard for you by getting men back behind the ball and defending in numbers. One of their main problems, and something I try to exploit when we play them, is the fact that if they go a goal behind they have to change their tactics. If they take the lead you know you are going to be in for a tough game because they become resilient and do not concede many goals. But I believe they find it difficult to come from behind.

However, it was a tremendous achievement to finish as high as they did in their first season back in the Premiership. I always felt Bryan would be looking to take things that one step further by acquiring a quality striker who can get them goals and it is another big coup for him to bring in Italian star, Fabrizio Ravanelli.

There has been something of an Italian influx in the Premiership and it will be interesting to see how they do in the new season. It is a great twist in the tale when you consider, not so long ago, it was everyone's ambition to play in Italian football. Now a lot of the top Italians are coming over here. I look on it as a great boost for the Premiership and long may it continue.

Last season Middlesbrough set out their stall. I am sure now a new front man has been brought in it will make them a lot more competitive, and possibly take them from mid-table to a position in the top eight.

In Steve Vickers they have an outstanding player. He was someone I watched very closely when he was at Tranmere, coming all the way through from the old Fourth Division. Bryan was brave in spending a lot of money on the Brazilian lads. Juninho has unbelievable potential but at the end of last season was still looking to make his mark in the Premiership.

I see certain similarities with Savo Milosevic because both lads are still very young and will have learned a great deal during their first season in English football. The arrival of Juninho shows they have

116

the desire to be competitive in the Premiership, but I think it may take longer to really establish themselves than it would for some of the bigger clubs.

NEWCASTLE UNITED

The first thing I have to say about my home town club is the fact that they have big Les Ferdinand and we haven't! They also have, of course, Alan Shearer!

Everyone knows I tried desperately hard to sign Les, but he chose Newcastle instead. He proved my judgement right by scoring a lot of goals in the Premiership last season – unfortunately, a couple of them against us. Maybe the fact that we wanted him proved to be the motivating force because in the two games against them I got the impression that Les was determined to show me what we had missed out on. Some players move on to so-called bigger clubs and never quite produce the form they have shown in the past. But, with no disrespect to QPR, Les moved on to a bigger platform and his game developed even more.

I think most managers in the country have the same view of Newcastle. They are brave, cavalier and exciting, even though so many people told Kevin Keegan not to play like that. I for one think it is brilliant that he had the guts to adopt that style. If that is what he believes in then that is what he has got to do.

The day Kevin succeeds, and believe me he will succeed, he will have every right to stand there, maybe not say a lot, but know that he has done it his way. When that day arrives, deep inside he will be glowing.

Already, he feels he has the talent at St James' Park to win honours and now, after capturing the country's number one striker in Alan Shearer, I happen to think he just might be right. I feel the experience of just missing out on the title last season may hold them in good stead for the future. You only have to look at Manchester United and what they have achieved since just missing out to Leeds in the title race a few years ago.

The other big plus for them is their crowd, which is almost as good as having an extra player on the park. In the eyes of the supporters, every throw-in, free kick, corner or goal kick is Newcastle's. Whenever we visit St James' Park, I always make sure I have a quiet word with the referee and remind him not to let the crowd referee the game, because all they see is black and white. I have friends and family who are season ticket holders at Newcastle and, believe me, they are absolutely fanatical. Because of that you almost wish success on the club.

NOTTINGHAM FOREST

If anyone had a hard job in football last season then it had to be Forest manager, Frank Clark. It was difficult enough a year earlier when he followed Brian Clough into the City Ground, especially after Forest had just been relegated. However, he stamped his authority on the team, did it his way and got them back into the Premiership, which was a fantastic achievement. But then to lose Stan Collymore was a real body blow. Stan had a phenomenal spell for Forest. It was always going to be difficult losing him and keeping the momentum going.

I am very friendly with Frank and speak to him regularly. I know for a fact that, even though he had his fair share of problems with Stan, he would take him back tomorrow if he could.

The way Forest play still has certain Cloughie characteristics. They get back behind the ball, see what you have to offer then, just when you feel you are getting on top of them, you find yourselves a goal down. That has been their style for some time now and Stan was so important because he was invariably the one who got them that vital goal.

Frank allows his front men to be just that. They do not go tracking back too far. They leave that job to the defenders who are quite happy to concede ground in midfield and let you go at them. Whenever we play Forest it is, again, one of those instances where I always tell my players not to over-commit themselves early doors. But after 15 minutes or so, when you might have had the better of the play and genuinely feel you can beat them, that is when they hit you. Generally, they are a very patient bunch of players and it is drilled into them to play a solid four at the back, four midfielders in front of them, and two up front with a bit of freedom.

Tactically they have not changed much over the years. When the opposition have the ball they are difficult to break down in the last third of the pitch. When Forest have the ball their wide players work the line and their strikers become target men to receive the ball and bring others into the play.

My favourite player at Forest has to be Colin Cooper, who was at Middlesbrough as a young lad when I worked there. Just watching him as a youngster playing alongside Gary Pallister and Tony Mowbray, it was no surprise to me that all three of them went on to become really good players, with Colin and Gary both gaining international honours. It was always a surprise to me that Tony did not follow suit. But for me Cooper is a real character, very determined in everything he does and a real 100 per center.

As a young kid he played at centre-back and then moved to full back. Now he is back as a central defender, and at Forest has blossomed into a tremendously talented player. The fact that Frank has held on to him is a great plus for Forest because the way they play they do rely a lot on defenders and Colin is one of the best in that role.

They are a side who are quite prepared to let the opposition get around the box and even shoot from 25 yards, believing that a defender will get in the way or the keeper will save it. Conceding ground but not conceding too many goals is a strange mix. However, it holds them in good stead and was probably one of the main reasons why they did well in Europe last season.

I have to say the Forest approach is the complete opposite to what I expect in a game. If we lose the ball I want it back as quickly as possible and I put huge demands on my forwards to chase back and close down opposition defenders when they are in possession. So when we play Forest there is a real contrast in styles. However, looking at the way they operate I am not surprised they twice nicked a late goal against us in the League last season to earn two draws.

SHEFFIELD WEDNESDAY

I nearly got involved with Wednesday towards the end of last season in the battle to sign Jon Newsome. He is a player I have always admired and there was some interest from me on a couple of occasions. But the fact that they signed him is one of the reasons why, in my opinion, they got themselves back together again after going through a difficult spell in the Premiership.

In David Pleat, Wednesday have a manager who is a purist. I have got to know David very well over the last few years. I followed him into Leicester and have played his teams so many times, first when he was at Luton and now against Wednesday.

He is a character who wants the ball to be passed around, and when his team are on their game they are always going to beat you. But his purism means that when it is not their day Wednesday often become quite easy to beat.

A lot of people have their philosophies on the game. I have often heard Glenn Hoddle say he will not change his methods and I am sure David thinks the same way.

Perhaps the biggest difference between David and myself is the fact that I am a result-orientated manager and he is a performance-orientated manager. When his teams are in form they are a delight to watch. They beat us 2-0 towards the end of the season and their performance on that occasion was outstanding. I am sure David would have been disappointed that they were unable to produce that type of display on a more regular basis.

Potentially, his team is exciting and he always produces good football side. I am sure being back in the Premiership last season will have taught him a lot and the arrival of Newsome will only be of benefit to them. But their undoing in the past has been their lack of consistency.

SOUTHAMPTON

They are a team who always seem to possess enough to stay in the Premiership. They are a hardened bunch when it comes to battling for survival and their achievement of staying in the top flight for so long is fantastic in many respects. Some teams, normally those who have just stepped up to the Premiership, lose a bit of heart if they suffer a few defeats. But Southampton are a side who always find that strength of character to get themselves out of trouble.

That is great credit to them especially as they have not been able to spend too much money over the past couple of seasons. Nevertheless, they are a good footballing side. Obviously, I cannot mention Southampton without talking about Matthew Le Tissier. Some of the things he does and some of the goals he scores are quite breathtaking, as we found to our cost a couple of seasons ago.

But no team can rely just on one player and I was beginning to wonder whether time was catching up on them when they pulled off a major coup by appointing Graeme Souness as their new manager. I sincerely hope they not only remain in the Premiership, but also make an impact under Graeme, even though I felt Dave Merrington did a very difficult job quite well last season.

There are not too many managers who win a domestic competition and then end up losing their job at the end of the season. That is what happened to Graeme at Turkish club, Galatasaray, who won their domestic cup under his leadership. He also won a lot of honours in charge at Rangers and the experiences of the past few years will possibly serve to make him an even better manager. His demands will be high and I am sure many will now expect Southampton to do a lot better than in previous seasons.

I have to say that in the past Saints have always been a different team at home compared to going away. The Dell seems to give them the belief that they can do well, and they produced the performance of last season by beating Manchester United so comprehensively. We were travelling up to Newcastle that day for our match at St James' Park the following afternoon. We knew that if United had beaten Saints it would have been virtually all over for Kevin Keegan's team. But when United lost we knew our task was going to be twice as difficult because, at the time, Newcastle were still in with a shout of winning the title.

That result at The Dell underlined the fact that on their day

Southampton can beat the best. And even if they do lose a few on the trot, they never lose sight of their final goal, which is survival. I always find Southampton a friendly club and, like I have said, I hope they do continue to win their battles, and stay in the Premiership for many seasons to come.

TOTTENHAM HOTSPUR

The big concern for me is that some day we are going to lose to Spurs. I remember Gerry Francis saying last season that he was pleased they only played us twice a year in the League, because we always beat them. As Villa manager I have been involved in three matches against Tottenham and we have won them all. But I have to say that the two meetings last season proved to be very close games.

Like their north London neighbours, Arsenal, Spurs are always very well organised and have clever defenders. They play a shrewd game and make it difficult for opposition strikers. Up front Chris Armstrong runs the line on his own a lot and he has been a terrific signing for them. He works the channels well, never lets defenders settle and, potentially, is an extremely good Premiership player. Teddy Sheringham is a class player as he demonstrated for England during this summer's European Championships. He drifts around and is difficult to pick up.

Tottenham's overall organisation has become one of their major strengths. They never give very much away, particularly on their travels. They have the ability to catch forwards offside, and can also slow the game down to their pace before hitting you when you least expect it, through Armstrong, Sheringham and Ruel Fox. Tactically, you have to try to press and worry their defenders, which is never the easiest thing to do. In many ways they have become similar to Arsenal in as much as their defenders are clever, their midfield players are functional and their forwards are always capable of hurting you.

When we played them last season I spent a lot of time with Ian Taylor encouraging him to come from deep and try to get beyond their defence. They produced some great results last season but, fortunately, from our point of view, we did well against them. Our tactics just gave us the upper hand and I only hope we can maintain our stranglehold over them in matches to come.

WEST HAM UNITED

Possibly West Ham's biggest strength is that in recent seasons they have thrown away their *Academy of Football* tag and become far more resilient and difficult to beat. I am not suggesting that they do not play good football any more – it is just that they have become very organised and have developed a strong desire not to lose matches.

There was a time when you associated West Ham with playing one way or no way at all, so to speak. But these days they have managed to combine the two facets of the game and that is probably why they enjoyed successful times last season. Ian Bishop and John Moncur are two strong midfield players who will always cause you problems if you do not get on top of them. Moncur has travelled quite a bit and did well at Swindon. But he has come on a lot at Upton Park and he and Bishop have developed a fine understanding. I remember West Ham beating Newcastle because those two guys ran the game.

Other big assets for West Ham are their manager, Harry Redknapp, who is a shrewd guy, and that very strong and determined full-back, Julian Dicks. I maintain that every player performs at his best when he finds somewhere he can call home and Dicks has found that at Upton Park. I see him as very much part of the club's future plans. If you were to ask the average West Ham supporter to pick his best team from the past few years it is a fair bet that Dicks would figure prominently.

Redknapp's signing of foreign players has also been good, with Bilic showing his strengths during the summer's European Championships. Upton Park has now become a difficult place to go and win. If I was hoping to expose any flaw then I would remind my players that, defensively, West Ham are not the quickest in the world. When we got the ball at their place we ran at them at every opportunity, and Dwight Yorke and Tommy Johnson caused them a fair amount of problems.

But they have spent money very wisely and to finish in the top half of the Premiership was a tremendous achievement.

WIMBLEDON

I do not think Wimbledon are quite as crazy as they like to make out. Deep down the players enjoy that image but there is nothing crazy about the way they keep producing exceptional talent and then make huge profits in the transfer market. That to me is a very shrewd operation.

When you play Wimbledon you know you have to have a competitive edge. We have been fortunate on the last couple of meetings at Villa Park because we have actually been more competitive than they have. When that is missing from their game it does make life a little easier for the opposition. But, overall, they are a difficult side to play against when they have everybody fit and well, especially when it comes to set pieces. Their corners and free kicks around the box always pose a threat and we know we have to be right on our game to counter them.

When we went to Selhurst Park last season the ever-enthusiastic Vinnie Jones was having a right go at us in the dug-out. There was an incident when the ball went out of play and one of our substitutes was warming up nearby. He did not pass the ball back and that really got to Vinnie, especially when I told him not to mouth of at our lad because it was not his job to be a ball boy. Inevitably, Vinnie gave me a mouthful but afterwards we had a laugh about it. He shook my hand and told me it was just part of game.

Actually, I quite like the fella. He knows his strengths and weaknesses and as a result has done very well in football. He is extremely competitive, winds his team mates up and is one of the main reasons why Wimbledon have done so well in staying in the Premiership over the years.

Of course, there is always the loud music in the home dressing room when you visit Selhurst Park to play Wimbledon. We take it with a pinch of salt, and try not to let it distract our preparations. There was a bit of that in the Villa dressing room when I first arrived.

It was something former Dons player, John Fashanu, had introduced but it was not my style so I soon got rid of it. But I respect Wimbledon because when they lose a game they get it out of their systems very quickly. They don't let it fester, they just think to themselves 'who are we playing next week, unlucky them'. That is a great mentality to have and there is a lot more talent about Wimbledon than many would like to admit.

THE NEWCOMERS

The Premiership newcomers this season are Derby County, Sunderland and my former club, Leicester City, who find themselves back in the big time after only one season away. As most people are aware, I still live in Leicestershire and the one thing I sensed throughout the area was that once Leicester reached the play-offs, they were going to get promoted. A lot of people were coming up and telling me that nothing was going to stop them from returning, and they were proved right.

I genuinely believe that their experiences of a year or so ago will help them this time. At the end of a season I have often spoken to managers whose team has been relegated, and they invariably say that if they could have the chance to start the season again they would survive, because of the knowledge they have picked up throughout the campaign. It is easy to analyse where you went wrong and you feel you could now go out and put it right, even with the same team. I know for a fact that was how Bolton manager Colin Todd felt at the end of last season when his side had just been relegated.

Psychologically, Leicester have a big advantage over the other two promoted teams in as much as they have players who have played in the Premiership, been relegated, and will have learned from the experience. They will come to terms with the fact that they will lose games during the season, but they will have more know-how about how to address the game after that, and so on. Some of the more experienced players at Filbert Street will be able to instill belief into their team mates and help them overcome any tough spells that may crop up.

I really hope Leicester do well enough to maintain their

Premiership status and I genuinely believe they will because playing against the likes of Manchester United, Liverpool, and even us, is still fresh in their minds. They will know what to expect.

As far as both Sunderland and Derby are concerned, it will be the psychological thing of how they can handle a defeat or two. I spoke to Sunderland manager, Peter Reid, during the summer and related one of my Leicester experiences to him. I told him I had only a small amount of money available at Filbert Street, but rather than spend it all I decided to keep some until around November, in case I needed a fresh player.

But the fact remains that once the season starts you need as strong a team as possible, so I told him I felt I was wrong in not going out and spending all my money before the campaign began. You know that if you do not start too well then you will be chasing the same type of player that the other strugglers around you will be looking at, and that makes the task all the harder. If you save some of your cash for a rainy day, once the rain comes you might not be able to attract the player you want because conditions are already too stormy.

Derby County manager Jim Smith, a tremendous character with more experience than most of us, will be very much aware of that as well. Jim was the manager who tried to sign me for Birmingham City for £600,000 many years ago, only for the deal to break down because of my back problems. He did a super job by getting Derby into the Premiership in his first season in charge at the Baseball Ground after selling quite a few of his big-name players.

So many people will pick Manchester United, Newcastle, Liverpool or hopefully ourselves for the title, with Derby, Leicester and Sunderland among the relegation favourites in the eyes of the average punter. But all three are potentially the same size and strength as a lot of the established teams in the Premiership, and I believe all three are quite capable of holding their own.

THE DEPARTURES

The three clubs we lost at the end of last season were, of course, Bolton, Manchester City and Queens Park Rangers. As I have said,

Colin Todd would love another chance based on what he learned last season. At times Bolton played some excellent football and came on very strong towards the end of the season. But on other occasions they were naive – the match against Manchester United sticking in the mind. They threw everything they could at United but then got punished because that is what top teams are capable of doing. They had some very good players and if they do bounce back first time then they will learn from such bitter experiences and probably use slightly different tactics to suit the occasion.

If you are looking for red-hot favourites to come straight back into the Premiership then, I suppose, you can look no further than Manchester City. But I have told quite a few people that I could have made a lot of money last season by having a bet that City would get relegated. Let me explain.

Back in the 1989-90 season when I was manager of Darlington in the GM Conference, we were beaten by Farnborough Town on my birthday. Later in the season they beat us again but were still relegated. Last season we went to Maine Road on my birthday and City beat us 1-0. In the return match at Villa Park City beat us again. In my 26 years in football only two teams have beaten me on my birthday and both ended up being relegated, so all you other teams had better beware!

In fairness, City caused us as many problems as any team we played last season. Uwe Rösler and Niall Quinn were outstanding, and a real handful for our defenders. Birthdays apart, I think a lot of people were surprised to see them get relegated, although with every season that comes up in future I guess a big club could find themselves in trouble. I am sure every Villa fan remembers only too well that we only just avoided going down the season before last. The First Division is difficult to get out of, as last season's favourites, Wolves, found out. But I think City have every chance of being back in the top flight at the beginning of next season.

QPR were always going to have difficulty surviving after losing the one player who could score goals regularly and keep them in with a chance of staying up. No one needs reminding that I am a big fan of the player I am referring to, Les Ferdinand. They badly missed that weapon who was capable of destroying you. But Rangers are a good footballing side and people enjoy watching them. They have the potential to figure in the promotion race and, as I have stated, that can also be said of both Bolton and Manchester City.

I hope my breakdown of the Premiership teams will give every Villa fan and every football supporter in general, an idea of what I will be looking for as the season unwinds.

Chapter Eleven

Behind The Scenes

Naturally, the most important feature of any football club is success on the pitch. While my prime aim is to try to ensure we win as many games as possible during a season, there are other aspects which are vital in helping make Aston Villa one of the biggest and, hopefully, one of the most successful clubs in the country.

While the chairman and I may be looked on as the highest profile figures at the club, many other people work tirelessly behind the scenes, providing tremendous back-up and support.

I have already talked briefly about my two assistants, Allan Evans and John Gregory, and how they form two corners of a triangle, underneath me. Normally, we work so that Allan and I are together, or John and me. It is rare that John and Allan work alongside each other because of the sheer nature of their individual jobs. During pre-season we have a period of physical work before we get down to the practical coaching side of things. When that begins it invariably means I am working more with John than with Allan.

John and I work with the midfield players and forwards, while Allan concentrates his thoughts towards the defenders at the club. I have to say that John and I bounce off each other very well. He usually starts the coaching sessions of attacking set-plays and formations, with me as the overseer. That does not mean that I ignore the defenders. I also get involved with them and add the bits I feel are necessary. Finally, after a gradual build-up in pre-season we reach the stage where we are playing 11-a-side training matches in preparation for the big kick-off.

John is a very bright, bubbly guy who is very demanding of players in as much as he is always seeking perfection. He gets very disappointed with players if he feels they are not performing to their best. Of course, John, Allan and I all played for Villa and we still like to join in sessions, hoping we can add something. I am probably the least effective, based on the fact that my back problems have left me less mobile than I would like, not to mention my two dodgy knees. But Allan and John are still fairly fit guys and have even played in our reserves on occasion last season.

The three of us have been together about five years. We have got to know each other so well that it normally needs only short conversations between us to know exactly what we want to do out on the training ground.

Just below Allan and John we have Kevin MacDonald and Tony McAndrew. Kevin had just a year with me at Leicester and another at Villa. Tony goes back further than any of the other three. He played under me at Darlington, was actually given a free transfer, but then returned to work with me as youth team coach.

Apart from one short break Tony has been with me around six years and has always been youth team coach. Tony is one of those guys I immediately turn to when I need an honest answer or opinion about anything. He is one of the few guys in the whole country I would turn to because he is such an honest person it is untrue. He has firm beliefs on certain issues and will always pick the right time and place to give me his views. As a result he is an extremely important and valuable member of my staff, a man of high principles, standards and disciplines, and definitely not afraid of hard work.

He gives the young kids good habits and that is very important. I maintain that if I buy a player of around 23 or 24 I will not be able to change his particular habits at that late stage of his development. The time to instill the good habits is when someone is 15 or 16, so the youth coach has a very important role to play in the life of a footballer. He can be an influence for the whole of a player's career. Some of you will have noticed that the kids at Villa often play a different system to the first team. That is because Tony's job is primarily to educate the youngsters how to play the game and operate in different positions.

Meanwhile, Kevin MacDonald has taken on the role of dealing with the young professional players who have progressed from the youth stage. That can be a difficult period for lads. Some of them can be knocking on the first team door at 18, while others are a bit slower in developing and may never make it at the highest level. But they still need coaching and pointing in the right direction. Over the years I have seen a lot of 18 to 20-year-olds lose a lot, because they find themselves with time on their hands. So we, like a lot of other football clubs, make sure we have a coach who spends a lot of time with these type of players.

Kevin's immediate directive is to help young professionals reach senior level. But if he is unable to do that with certain individuals who may not quite be good enough, then his next directive is to make sure they can make themselves a good living in the game, albeit outside the Premiership. Over the last 12 months or so we sold David Farrell to Wycombe Wanderers, Trevor Berry to Rotherham, Stephen Cowe to Swindon and Chris Boden to Derby County. Our feelings were that if they were not going to make it as first team players at Villa, then they could still make a living elsewhere, and Kevin played a big part in their development.

One of the guys I inherited when I became Villa manager was Paul Barron, a fitness specialist and former goalkeeper who is now a fully qualified goalkeeping coach. When I arrived at the football club there was, naturally, a degree of uncertainty for all the backroom staff already there. But I soon discovered that Paul was a very willing volunteer who would come to me and ask what was to be done. By contrast, you may recall I mentioned Colin Clarke in a previous chapter and the fact that there was very little communication between us. Paul was just the opposite and has since gelled very well with the rest of the coaching staff.

In fact, when I came to the club Paul was only here on a consultancy basis and was not a full time member of the staff. But that has since changed because of the attitude he has shown under me. He is also allowed to do work for the English Schools FA, which is an important role for him and also good for our club to have an 'in' to the England set-up. Paul has not only worked well with the goalkeepers but has also helped us work out the fitness level of each player at the club. He and physio Jim Walker spent a lot of time preparing the right diet and I feel we have now perfected that to the benefit of the players as well as any other club in the country.

The players now accept that Paul and Jim are telling them things for their own good and they respond accordingly. If they are given an energy drink or certain type of food, or even handed a working schedule for the gymnasium, they know they are being given it for the right reasons rather than just for the sake of it. I have to admit that Paul and Jim have taken this aspect of their work on to a plane which, at times, is even above me. I allow them that freedom because their methods are proving to be the right ones.

There has often been talk that European players, particularly the Italians, are miles ahead of us in such matters. But I genuinely feel that in this country we have now developed ways of getting the best out of individuals and also shown them how they can get the best out of themselves.

For example, some of you may find it strange to know that we invariably work quite hard the day after a game, particularly if we have a run of matches in a short period of time. We often call all the lads in the day after a match and let them go for a run, because that now appears to be the best way to get some of the stiffness out of limbs after a tough game the previous night.

Paul and Jim have studied the methods we use and their contribution has proved very beneficial in what I am trying to achieve at the club. So, overall, I feel we have a great mix in the coaching staff. We all get on exceptionally well with one another when it comes to work, although the one thing I do not encourage is to be living in each other's houses when the work stops. That is not necessary, although we class ourselves as friends, which is important in finding harmony and understanding.

I am only too aware that within the framework we have built there could be a time when someone wants to move on and do his own particular thing elsewhere. Allan, John and I have formed a team for the best part of five years and I genuinely hope we stay together for a long time to come. But, having said that, I am now about to contradict myself by accepting that if one of them, or any other member of the backroom staff, decided he wanted to move on then I would not stand in his way. As the manager, I can do what I want to do, and I am aware that others around me have ambitions and may one day want the sort of freedom that I have.

Throughout the relationship between the three of us, Allan and John have always been encouraged to voice their opinions. We normally have a monthly staff meeting to discuss the playing side of things, right from schoolboy football, through the youth and reserves to senior level, as well as physiotherapy, fitness and scouting reports. Rest assured, that during the course of conversation there have been one or two moments of disagreement, which can only be expected when a number of people sit around a table and express their personal views. But we make sure that it never goes outside the four walls and I have to admit that I have the final say, and the rest accept that. But, overall, we are very much together.

There is an unbelievable amount of trust between us and I genuinely feel that not one of my staff would slag me off, either publicly or behind my back. We are all different characters, but I sense the players can see we are a group who have gelled together. If a player does something and one of the coaching staff finds out about it, then they know it will also get back to me because that is the way we operate. When it comes to matters of work we do not keep secrets from each other.

Peter Withe will always be remembered for his winning goal for Villa in the European Cup Final 14 years ago. Peter now has the very important role of Youth Development Officer at the club. He is at the head of a massive operation dealing with schoolboy football with an age range from nine to 14.

We have a scouting system covering the whole country as well as Scotland, Northern Ireland and the Irish Republic. As well as scouts we have spotters who recommend lads to the scouts. It is a very competitive market trying to find the youngsters who, in the long

133

term, may save you millions in the transfer market. We already have three Schools of Excellence and soon we hope to have a residential school so that the lads can have lessons in the day time and be coached at night.

I believe this is the way better players will be produced in this country. If a youngster can practise every night with the assistance of qualified coaches he is bound to get better. Peter is the overseer and I am sure one day he might even find the new Peter Withe.

Malcolm Beard is my chief scout and we also go back a long way. We worked together at Middlesbrough and Leicester, and now he has joined me at Villa. The relationship with Malcolm is different from the rest in as much that he works more for me rather than for the football club as a whole. Although he is in charge of the overall scouting side of things we work very close to each other.

He knows the sort of things I am looking for in the game and his team assessments prove invaluable to me. Quite often I don't go and see a team before we are due to play them. Invariably, Malcolm has taken a look at them at least twice, sometimes more than that.

I mentioned in a previous chapter about the way Leeds manager, Howard Wilkinson, often picks his team based on the strengths and weaknesses of the opposition. I rarely watch a team just before we play them but rely on the report that Malcolm produces for me. I like to watch the opposition when it suits me. For example, I might go and take a look at a team in September when we are not due to play them until November. That way I do not get too influenced by their style even though I have been able to assess them. Nearer the game itself Malcolm runs the rule over the opposition and that is why he plays such an important role.

Apart from being at the training ground I also spend a lot of time at Villa Park. I have to say that the telephone is not my favourite piece of equipment, as valuable as it can be at times. I am the type of person who likes to see things. By being at the ground I see and hear things that I might otherwise miss. I like to see how departments work, even how individuals work, and things that do not directly involve me. When I was at Darlington I more or less ran the club and towards the end of my managerial spell at Leicester I had a say in virtually everything that was going on. Here at Villa my role is team manager but that does not stop me from wanting to know about the administration side, the commercial side, or whatever.

The whole thing is a massive operation, but I have made sure I have found out how each area functions. Now, two years down the road, I am pleased that I know what is going on generally within the club. Putting a team out on a Saturday is a difficult enough operation in itself and, at times, a big headache. But if my role stopped there then I do not think I would be getting true job satisfaction. So I strive to have an input into anything and everything that goes on at the football club.

I often pop into the office of commercial manager, Abdul Rashid, for a 10-minute chat, likewise with club secretary, Steve Stride. Some days there is nothing going on, but on other occasions it is surprising what I suddenly find myself involved in.

Even when it is one of those quiet days I invariably go into the chairman's office for a chat and a cup of tea. Some of you may find that strange, particularly as Mr Ellis has built a reputation over the years that has now earned him the nickname of 'Deadly Doug'. But I don't find it a problem. In fact, I have to say that I quite enjoy the experience. We can have serious conversations about what is going on, but there are times when we also have a good laugh. During the time I have been at Villa I feel the relationship between the two of us has developed enormously.

I have known the chairman since I first came into football and I don't think the word 'fear' has ever come into my thinking about any-one, least of all Mr Ellis. If people have tried to frighten me in the past they have had little response. I find it quite funny that people call the chairman 'Deadly' and even try to avoid him in some instances. Actually, I go out of my way to make sure I see him most days and although I feel that is a very important role for me to play, I can assure all the doubters that it is not an act. The chairman is always interest-ed in my thoughts and I have no worries about relaying those thoughts to him.

When I first came to Villa as manager I know criticism was levelled at the chairman with suggestions that by employing me he had brought in his 'yes' man. All I can say is that those comments are so way off the mark they are laughable. Anyone who knows me realises that of all the people who has a mind of his own, I am probably top of the list in that respect. Just because I don't stand there bawling and shouting at people, does not mean that I am a soft touch who does not have a mind of my own and can be ordered around. As a player I was always stubborn and I still maintain that streak in me.

My beliefs have led me into both good and bad things. However, unless anyone can genuinely convince me that what I am doing is wrong then I will never change my ways just for the sake of it. When I was a player I lost my loyalty bonus year after year because I felt I was right in speaking out and saying certain things to people that was obviously not what they wanted to hear.

When I first arrived here I saw quite a few letters in the local Press expressing the opinion that the chairman had brought in his puppet. Maybe some of the letters were written by younger people who did not remember me as a player. But some of the initial response really disappointed me, and I hope I have now convinced some of the doubters otherwise. The chairman is Villa through and through but he knows that if I do not agree with something he says I will tell him and him alone. I would not stand there in public and criticise the chairman and I certainly would not say it behind his back because I feel that is not the right thing to do.

But if I think something needs to be said I have no fears about telling him. And as a result it appears he has now seen another side of me that perhaps he did not know existed before I became his team manager. Yes, he was brave in bringing me in, and there was a short period when, maybe, it did not look as though it was the right thing to do. However, if it had gone wrong in that initial spell it would have been MY fault not his, that's for sure.

There have been times when I have needed his shoulder to lean on. I remember vividly how down and depressed I was after we were beaten 4-0 by Arsenal the season before last. Afterwards I sat on my own in the coaches' room at Villa Park and, credit to the chairman, he came in and had a chat to me. Other chairmen might have thought it best to avoid their manager at a time like that. But he sat down with me for 10 minutes or so and, seeing how down I was, he suggested all of us should go away for a few days' break.

He said 'come on, we will all go away for three or four days, get together, do a bit of training if you like, but just get away from everything and everyone for a while'. So he booked 20 seats on a flight to Majorca and off we went to prepare ourselves for the final three games of the season which, in the end, proved to be enough to ensure we avoided relegation. But I reckon to this day he could see how depressed I was after the Arsenal defeat, and he organised the trip just as much for my benefit as for the players, so credit to him.

So I have already seen that he was prepared to give me some help when I needed it and, apart from the financial backing I have received, it is nice to know that other types of support are there if ever I require them in future. Three weeks after our break in Majorca we drew at Norwich to stay in the Premiership. I could see how drained the chairman was, even though he was also very relieved that we had survived. That was when I was able to give him a bit of support, by giving him a hug and reassuring him, a bit tongue-in-cheek, that I knew it would all come out right in the end.

Last summer we had a meeting and he told me I had anything up to £8m to spend and again, credit to him, he never tried to influence me on how best to spend it. By the same token, he has never tried to pick my team for me. However, I often go into him and talk about the game that has just gone, or the one that is coming up, and I think he appreciates that. Also, he never criticises me if I change my mind. Sometimes a few days before a match I will tell him how I think it is best to tackle the job. Then the day before the match I may have changed my mind.

In some walks of life a boss might wonder if his employee knows what he is talking about if that were to happen, but football it totally different to anything else. The chairman accepts that, and if I make one decision one day and another one the next then there are no questions asked. I can release my emotions to the chairman and, as a result, he has got to know me better as a person rather than just as a football manager. And I talk to him like I would talk to one of my assistants, keeping him informed on what I am doing. I do not keep secrets from him. As a result, he probably appreciates the fact that he feels part of everything that is taking place on the footballing side of things.

By the same token, I have learned a lot from him. When we have conducted big transfer deals, like the one with Partizan Belgrade for Savo Milosevic, I have seen how he operates and that has given me a deeper insight into him as a person and not just as the chairman of the football club. Overall, our relationship has developed into a strong one. Of course, at some stage it may go wrong. We are all aware of what can happen in football because that is the nature of the game. The job could go wrong for me one day, as it could for any manager. But I don't think it would damage the sort of relationship we have built.

When we are in a room together we are able to talk openly and frankly to one another, and to me that is a very important relationship. We understand each other. I am not so sure that is a very common thing in football these days. But I believe that is the best way. I see little point in hiding anything from the man who has the ultimate say in how he sees the football club developing and how he feels it should develop. I can develop the team under the guidelines I am given. Even in the past if a chairman has come up to me and said that he didn't want to do this or that, then I would work within that framework publicly. That is why it is vital I know how the chairman is thinking. In that respect going to Villa Park so often has been a very worthwhile exercise.

The chairman tends to have a similar type of relationship with each head of department. He and Steve Stride work very closely together on the whole administration side of the club and Abdul Rashid has many meetings with the chairman about what has to be done on the commercial side.

That is very different to my days at Leicester where the nine-man board would meet and then split off into sub-committees to investigate any particular aspect of the club before reporting back to a full board meeting sometime in the future.

Here at Villa we have a fairly small board of directors and, as a result, the chairman is the man who can make the decisions. So meetings with him enable the heads of departments to know in which direction they can go. Mr Ellis is very much the father figure at Aston Villa who makes the ultimate decisions. That helps make the whole running of the club a fairly simple operation in that respect.

One of the roles I have to undertake as manager of Villa is regular meetings with the Press. When I first took the job it was custom and practice for local and national journalists, as well as radio and television guys, to assemble at our Bodymoor Heath training ground on a Friday lunch time or the day before a midweek match. That enabled them to carry out interviews with myself and some of the players. I decided to end that procedure. Some of the Press people I deal with regularly suggested it was because they had given me a bit of a hard time when we were going through that sticky patch the season before last.

That was not the reason at all. I have already mentioned that I look on the training ground as a place for serious work. My job is all about preparing for games and winning games, and anything that may affect those preparations has to be dealt with. In my first few months at the club I appreciated the importance of the Press, so when they turned up for interviews I would stop what I was doing and go and meet them. It also meant that the media were in amongst the players little more than 24 hours before a big game, talking about the match. I just felt it was all becoming too much of a distraction.

As a result I told the Press that any interviews with players would be brought forward by 24 hours – in other words, two days before a match. This gave the players more time to prepare themselves mentally for the task ahead, concentrate on what they had to do on the pitch, rather than think about what they had to say if a microphone was thrust in front of them.

A lot of my players are still fairly young, and to a degree they 'act' a bit if they see a camera focused in their direction, or if they talk to a Press guy. Sometimes they might even say things that they don't really want to say. They are not 100 per cent aware of what they might say can be interpreted or even misinterpreted.

So, although there was some form of protection, the bottom line for me was the fact that the training ground is the place where players go to work and the fewer distractions the better. In a way I set myself up to be shot down because if results had not improved with the new system then, no doubt, I would have been asked why I was doing it. But the fact that last season our results did improve showed to me that there were some benefits in keeping the players away from the media the day before a game. As for myself, I still meet the Press the day before a match but those meetings now take place at Villa Park after all my work at the training ground has been completed.

The demands of the media are very high. You only have to look at the different areas of the Press to realise it is never a particularly easy operation to deal with them. There is local radio, national radio, local television, national television, Sky TV, national sports writers, feature writers, Sunday newspaper guys, and those from the local morning and evening newspapers. Each one is looking for a slightly different angle to a story and, of course, for the exclusive.

Some of them think they have a divine right to a story because of who they are, or who they work for. That has sometimes meant I have had a few run-ins and arguments with certain individuals over the last year or so. Dealing with the Press can be quite a strain and took a bit of getting used to because I believe it is very important how I, my staff and players portray Aston Villa publicly.

I received quite a lot of criticism in the early days at the football club and I tried to look at it objectively, although there were times when it did hurt quite a bit.

Sometimes I asked myself whether I deserved that type of story levelled at me. I suppose when I read a story about someone else which is, perhaps, a bit hurtful, I tend to dismiss it fairly quickly because it does not directly involve me. So when it is actually me under the cosh from the Press I try to put things into perspective and think that there are a lot of people out there who are not particularly bothered about what has been said. Some take it in, some don't. But I have to admit that I am one of those guys who much prefers receiving praise rather than taking stick.

A lot of people in the game have told me that getting a bit of criticism brings the best out of them. I really do not know how anyone can say that. It certainly is not the case as far as I am concerned.

In my playing days if I got slaughtered and felt it was unjustified then that particular journalist would not get a lot more out of me. I did not expect people to give me a load of 'bull' about how well I had played but ,generally, I just liked Press guys to be polite to me.

These days I understand what is behind some of the stories because everyone is trying to make them more dramatic to try to win the readership war. The newspaper business is a very competitive market. But it concerns me when I see a story being printed that contains little or no substance. I am not talking about the actual match reports, because if your team plays badly you have to accept it. Criticism of how you play is part and parcel of a game. But when it becomes more personal, that is when it can get a bit hurtful.

There were quite a few letters in the local newspapers in the early days suggesting I was not the right man for the job. I have kept copies of most of them tucked away in a drawer at work. I also have a framed copy of the infamous press statement when I left Leicester City. That is just something very personal. But some of the letters I have kept to act as motivation for me. They help me keep myself straight. When events are going well I often take them out and read them, if only make sure I keep my feet on the ground. When things are moving along nicely it does not do any harm to remind yourself, now and again, that things can go wrong and not to get too carried away.

Chapter Twelve

In The Dressing Room

As you have probably gathered by now I have to be organised in my work and an organised dressing room is more important than anything else as far as I am concerned.

I have always adopted a policy in my dressing room of sticking to good habits. The one guy who reminds me more than anyone else about the standards I keep is Dwight Yorke. He often walks up to me, and with one of those big smiles says: "I know, gaffer, good habits."

I have always maintained that after I had just joined Villa as a kid, I had all sorts of good habits, rules and regulations instilled into me. They came first from Graham Leggatt, who was my youth team coach for a short spell, and then more especially from Frank Upton.

So, despite being a player with long hair, I still felt I was a creature of good habits. I learned how to look after my boots and keep them well polished. I learned how to change studs. I made sure I was well dressed when I represented the football club, even if it was kipper ties and flared trousers in those days.

Some people have asked me if I picked up any good habits from former Villa manager, Ron Saunders, who everyone looked on as a very strict disciplinarian. Let me say that football was a bit different in those days compared with what it is today. There was only one substitute when Ron was in charge, so that meant he was interested in maybe only 12 or 13 players at any one time. By comparison, it is very much a squad game these days. In Ron's era, when I was a player, if you were not in that select first team party you were very much out of the picture. You even wore a different coloured jersey for training.

I remember vividly how sometimes a player would walk out with a blue first team training top on and the kit man would be sent out to take it off him, in front of all his team mates, because he was not involved in the senior squad that particular day. I know that used to destroy quite a few of the established first team players at that time. Once that coveted blue top had been taken off you on Ron's orders then you knew you would not be in the first team that weekend. Fortunately, it never happened to me, although I had quite a few arguments with him about other matters over the years.

Having said that, I feel there are certain aspects of my managerial style that have some of his characteristics. I am sure that cannot be a bad thing. I probably understand and respect him more today than ever I did as a player.

At times he was difficult to fathom out, to say the least. But when you are a bit older, maybe, you look back and realise he was doing things for the best. After all, he was a very successful manager, so you cannot really argue against his methods. He knew what he wanted and he knew how to get it. Hopefully, that is something I learned from him.

I have now been manager at three different clubs. I went to Darlington when they were bottom of the old Fourth Division. I moved to Leicester after they had finished as low as they ever had in the old Second Division, and I came to Villa when they were in their lowest position for a few years. On each occasion I felt that the dressing room was the place where things were not quite ticking over as well as they should have been. More often than not, the manager is the person who gets the sack and, obviously, it was the dismissal of Ron Atkinson that led to me coming here. But I think the players have a mighty big part to play in success or failure.

How they behave in the dressing room, how they approach their work in terms of training and the playing of matches, often determines whether a manager is going to do well at a particular club. All managers have different ideas. Mine are based on my upbringing in the game. So one of my most important rules is good time-keeping. If I am travelling anywhere I do everything I can to make sure I am on time. I expect the same from my players and much prefer them to be even a bit early when it comes to turning up for training, matches or any other functions. For example, if someone tells you the team coach leaves at 10.15, I don't expect anyone to be jumping on it just as it is pulling away.

So at each of the clubs where I have been manager I have compiled a list of rules and regulations that I believe helps teach my players good habits. I am talking about things like making sure they go into the showers wearing flip-flops. Let's face it, feet are the most important part of any footballer's body in many respects. So the last thing you want is athlete's foot, or to stand on a piece of glass or sharp metal, or anything else that could cause damage and force you to miss an important match. I hate seeing players walk around barefoot, and as they will not be wearing boots in the dressing room all the time flip-flops are important.

Other things I insist on include making sure players are not unshaven on match days, the wearing of smart clothes, and a generally tidy approach. I know some of you will remember that I always played with my shirt outside my shorts and I did have a beard once, but I look back and realise I was wrong at the time and I am big enough to admit it.

So whatever rules and regulations I introduce I expect them to be carried out. When we are out on the training ground and the public have turned up to watch us the last thing I want to hear is one of my players swearing out loud. In the heat of the dressing room on a match day I suppose I swear as much as anyone. We have all seen the famous Graham Taylor video, and although he is not alone in the words he came out with there is no way I want to hear someone swearing in public, especially when there could be youngsters nearby watching us.

It also annoyed me when I first came to Villa that a player would often take off a tracksuit top during training and then leave it on the ground at the end of the session expecting one of the YTS lads to go and fetch it. Why should a young kid be expected to walk all the way to the far side of the training ground just because a professional had been too lazy to do his own tidying up?

So within a few days of my arrival at the club I introduced a load of rules, some of them silly little ones but, nevertheless, ones I felt would help make the players better people. I made sure they knew I wanted things done in a certain way. When it was written down in black and white for them and stuck up on the wall for all to see there could be no argument.

Every time someone broke one of the rules he was fined the princely sum of £5. In fairness to some of the guys, a fiver was not going to hurt them too much. But if they stepped out of line then they received an official letter informing them of the fine. If they happened to swear at a coach during training then that would cost them £10. I know a lot of them hated the thought of being fined, even £5, but it happened because they just could not help themselves.

Amazingly, Dean Saunders was probably fined more times than the rest of the lads put together. It was just a case of him being 30-something and already set in his ways. He was the type who never thought about putting on his flip-flops, picking up his track suit top after training or even parking his car in the correct place at the training ground. That was another 'offence' that caught out a lot of players. They parked as close to the dressing rooms as they could, possibly because they had arrived with only minutes to spare, or they thought they were all set for a quick getaway after training. Whatever the reasons I soon made sure they did park in the proper place. If they did not then they knew they would be handing over another fiver.

Just in case anyone thought I was keeping the cash myself let me explain that it was all retained until Christmas, then we would buy presents and let the players distribute them to children in a local hospital. It was surprising how the money mounted up during the first few months of the fines being introduced. Some people would say that the fines did not make players any better footballers. But I would argue that it did not make them any worse footballers.

When I was a player I remember one of my team mates, Gary Shaw, standing on a short nail when he was not wearing anything on his feet. He missed a game because of it. So what is the point of a player taking off his boots and walking across a training ground in only his socks? Someone could easily have broken a bottle on the ground the previous night, and that could cause untold damage.

Another of my early rules was that there would be no gambling on the team coach travelling to and from away matches. I honestly felt players would not be in the right frame of mind to play a game if they had just lost quite a bit of money playing cards on the way to the ground. Gambling is something that really concerns me. I have seen a lot of it over the years and I do not like it very much. When I was a player the furthest I ever went in that direction was to have a 50p Yankee on the horses.

I like horse racing, greyhound racing and even a game of cards. I do not mind playing cards for a pound coin. But I hate the idea of anyone playing cards and, maybe, losing £100 or more just before they turn their attentions towards playing a match. Surely they cannot be properly prepared for the job in hand knowing they have just lost a large amount of money?

But having just revealed to you about my rule making I am now about to contradict myself by saying that a year or so down the road, after I had imposed my influence on the dressing room, I decided to virtually scrap all the rules I had put into place.

At the beginning of last season I called all the players together and told them that they would no longer be fined for not wearing flip-flops, parking their cars in the wrong place and they could even play cards on the coach again if they wished. As I made the statement I could see some of the players' jaws dropping so much in disbelief they almost hit the ground. I told them that they now knew how I thought and what I liked, so just make sure they did not disappoint me. I made it clear that even though the rules had been relaxed I did not expect them to fall back into any bad habits.

The most pleasing aspect for me is the fact that, nowadays, they do wear flip-flops rather than walk about bare foot; they do pick up their training kit and keep it tidy; and they do turn up for matches clean shaven and smart. They are even polite enough to take off baseball caps when they walk into the dining area at the training ground because they know that is what I expect. In fairness, I have to say that during last season I had a fantastic response from them as a group of people.

However, there was one rule I did keep and made it clear to them that if it was broken it would cost them far more than just a fiver. I explained that if they turned up late for training they would be docked a minimum of five per cent of their weekly wage. Suddenly I had gone from the light fivers to the big heavy stuff. I also pointed out that although they could play cards on the team coach, that would stop immediately we were on our way from the team hotel to the ground we were visiting. It is quite funny now, because if ever I walk down the team coach on a long journey I can see the lads quickly stop playing cards and pretend to be doing something else instead.

Another thing that has always annoyed me is that well-worn piece of equipment, the mobile phone. I have to say that despite all my other dislikes they come very near the top of the list even though I have to use one myself on many occasions. However, when I became Villa manager it seemed every player at the club had a mobile phone and thought it was all right to use it at any time. I would walk into the dressing room five minutes before training and there was someone sitting there talking away on his phone. There is no way that person could have been concentrating on going out and doing some important training.

In the dining room after training the players would not be talking to each other. Instead they would be talking to someone on the phone. Sometimes I would be sitting on the team coach going to a game and suddenly mobile phones would be ringing left, right and centre. As soon as we had finished a match, whatever the result, they would be ringing again. As a result I banned mobile phones from work with the only exception being if someone needed to use one in an emergency, but only in an emergency. Otherwise, as soon as a player enters the gates of the training ground, the mobile phones are switched off and packed away out of my sight.

Our training ground at Bodymoor Heath is one of the best equipped in the country, but I was rather concerned when I took charge of the football club to discover that there was a recreation room in the complex that had large comfortable seats and two table-tennis tables. I noticed that five minutes before training was due to begin players were still playing table tennis or lounging around on the settees, probably using their mobile phones. Now the one thing I am sure about is that table tennis is not going to make anyone a better footballer.

All right, some might argue that it would improve reflexes, but I certainly did not see it that way. So I decided the space would be best utilised as a multi-gym area, and we now have around £100,000 worth of high quality equipment for the players to work on. Fitness coach Paul Barron has a work-out chart for each player, and he and physio Jim Walker combine to make sure everything is properly used.

These days players often come in an hour before training is due to start to do a session. I would say that 90 per cent of our players now use the multi-gym, day in, day out, while the other 10 per cent use it when they feel it suits them. Overall, they appreciate they have access to equipment and facilities that they would normally only find at a top leisure centre and would probably have to pay a lot to use. It has proved particularly beneficial to players who have picked up injuries. We can now treat them even better on the spot rather than send them off to Lilleshall, or wherever, for rehabilitation.

I have found habits have changed, and as a result I am convinced team spirit has improved. If someone does let a swear word slip out on the training ground I invariably get an apology straight away. I have also noticed that if we are playing a match and the opposition skipper walks into our dressing room wearing only socks, then our lads look at him in disbelief, knowing he could stand on something dangerous or even stub his toe just before an important game.

So, as you can imagine, there has not only been a lot of major surgery as far as buying and selling is concerned, but also a good deal in the dressing room. Now I feel the lads who carried us to victory in the Coca-Cola Cup, helped us reach the FA Cup semi-finals, and finished fourth in the Premiership, deserve to take us, hopefully, that next step forward.

I believe all the major surgery has been completed for the time being. Now all we require is a bit of fine tuning. Of course we need to stay fairly injury free. No team can carry lots of injuries, as we found to our cost towards the end of last season. But in the main I have a group of players who want success and know how their manager and his staff are thinking and, in many respects, want to please us.

Yes, we did achieve something last season but that does not mean we start doing different things and falling back into bad habits. It is important everyone realises there can only be one chief and the indians follow him. It is no good having six or seven chiefs in the dressing room in the new season. I am the one who will still be making the decisions and I expect my players to accept them. At times they may not understand what I am asking of them. But if they believe in me and my staff then I think the base is there for good things in the future.

I suppose every player has his own particular character and it is generally recognised that one of the hardest parts of a manager's job is what is generally known as man-management. I again look back on my days as a player and believe that Ron Saunders, Vic Crowe and Tommy Docherty held the philosophy that they had a certain plan that was going to work on anybody and everybody. But I remember when I was yelled at, the manager would lose me for a while as far as work was concerned. I used to wonder what was the point of someone having a go at me. It was not as if I was trying to make mistakes on purpose.

Of course, there are times when I yell at an individual. But more often than not I then follow that up with a load of praise and confidence-building comments to try to ensure they put it right next time. I maintain that no player ever goes out on a match day to play badly and deliberately make mistakes. But mistakes are bound to happen some time. So the fact that I can accept them without bawling someone's head off helps make me the type of manager I am. Encouragement can be far more valuable than criticism. If I do criticise then I try to make constructive, rather than destructive comments.

Perhaps the one player who responded to that more than anyone else last season was Dwight Yorke. I see Dwight's temperament as similar to mine as a player. He needs to be encouraged, needs to have someone believe in him and be told that he is a good player who is wanted. But at the same time I have to be strong enough to give him that little kick up the backside if I feel it is necessary. I do a lot of my work with Dwight in quiet moments, talking to him about his game, giving him my views, reminding him who he is playing against in the next match or how he got on against his marker in the previous game.

I encourage him to prey on the opposition weaknesses and play to his own strengths. I think that has helped him come on one hell of a lot over the last 12 months or so. A lot of people look on Dwight as a shy guy, but I have to say that, in many respects, he is probably the biggest show-off in my team when it comes to being out on the pitch. Now it has even spread to the dressing room because he loves to hear his song sung, 'Start Spreading the News... Dwight Yorke, Dwight Yorke'.

After we won the Coca-Cola Cup at Wembley most of the lads had gone upstairs for a drink with friends and family and there were only a few of us left in the dressing room, including Dwight. He was sitting in the corner singing 'his song' at the top of his voice. I thought that was fantastic.

Last season was a super one for him and I think he has responded as well as anyone to the way I work. I don't mind him showing off a bit if he continues to play as he has been. During last season I revealed how he stood in a bin in the middle of the dressing room, keeping a ball up on his head. So don't ever think Dwight is one of those shy people. The football field is a stage and I love it when he goes out there and becomes the showman.

If we are looking for real extroverts in the dressing room then we need look no further than our keeper, Mark Bosnich. I first saw Bozzie play for Aston Villa reserves against Leeds at Elland Road a few years ago while I was still manager of Leicester City. I remember watching this guy and asking myself why he did not move from the centre of his goal. His positional sense seemed hopeless. But then he kept diving up into the top corner, or down by a post, and saving everything. I realised he was actually encouraging the opposition to shoot at him so he could show them what he could do.

Bozzie must have only been about 20 at the time, but I remember being quite amazed by his performance. I was taken aback by it all.

Villa won 2-0, yet Bozzie must have saved about 20 shots. So it came as no surprise to me that a couple of years later he was a first team regular at Villa Park. He has improved tremendously, as far as positional sense is concerned, and also has unbelievable athleticism in the goalmouth. Apart from being a very good goalkeeper he is also quite a character.

A couple of days before a match Bozzie will start predicting the score and telling the rest of the lads that he will not be letting in any goals. He has this positive attitude, but instead of telling everyone once or twice what the score will be, he just goes on and on about it. So in the dressing room, while he is shouting out his prediction, you can hear the other lads snoring, pretending he is sending them to sleep. But that doesn't put Bozzie off. He just gets worse because of it. Even on the team coach, when he starts all over again, everyone just lies down and shuts their eyes. So, as you can imagine, Bozzie is the brunt for quite a bit of the humour that goes on in the dressing room. But he is so thick-skinned and has such a strong personality that he just brushes it all aside.

When I arrived at Villa it has to be said that Bozzie was going through a bit of an indifferent spell. We had a few early meetings to try to sort things out and maybe there was a bit of sparring going on between the two of us. He was unsure of me and was still very young, in terms of goalkeeping, and how far he had come in such a short time. Most keepers do not reach maturity until they are considerably older than him. Villa were also going through a bad spell and he had a lot of responsibility on his shoulders and that may have tested him a bit.

Being a youngster he was probably looking for reasons why things were not going to plan but he did not have the experience to come up with the right answers. It was an awkward period for him. But Bozzie has learned from the experience and become a stronger character because of it. As time has gone by he has grown into someone I would now have no hesitation in confiding in, such is our relationship.

In a similar sort of way Mark Draper was tested by being a member of a side at Leicester who found themselves struggling and eventually relegated from the Premiership after only one season, although they are now back in the top flight. I am sure the experience of battling for survival will hold Mark in good stead for the future. But as a person Mark is another one who is the life and soul of the dressing room.

Like the rest of the players he knows when it is time to work, but in the more relaxing moments he is always laughing. When you consider Mark's two seasons before the last one – getting relegated at Leicester and then finding himself in a struggling team at Villa – he has managed to come through that, still with a smile on his face.

Mark has a burning ambition to be successful but at the same time he is a happy person you cannot help but like. I remember him once coming into my office and telling me he was going to ask me three favours. He asked me the first and second and I agreed to both. Then he just sat in the chair opposite me with a blank look on his face. When I asked him what the third favour was he just stared at me and said: "I can't remember, gaffer!" In the end he was laughing at himself and that just about sums him up.

I believe 'Drapes' is as talented as any player in this country. When I first signed him for Leicester I remember watching him during training and thinking to myself that he was so much better than anyone else I had got. He really is a superbly talented guy. He did very well for us last season and there were times when he was absolutely outstanding. A lot of us felt he could so easily have broken into the England reckoning.

Naturally, Terry Venables had set ideas, and after coming through the European Championships with flying colours he could not be criticised about his choice of players. But now there is a new guy at the helm in Glenn Hoddle. I believe Mark will do even better for us in the seasons that lie ahead and could well break into the international squad.

But I would not want him to change his ways. He is just a happy lad, very funny and very talented. As a football manager I come across some players who are quite hard work when it comes to conversation. But he likes to have a chat and when the time is right he always has a smile on his face. He would be very close to being as popular as anyone in the dressing room..

There was an awful lot of change at Villa within a few months of my arrival, with the Press making a lot of the fact that some of the older players were being moved out to be replaced by younger ones. That was the theme they adopted and, in many instances, tried to make mountains out of mole hills. As you are aware, some of the more experienced players did stay, including Nigel Spink, for a while, Steve Staunton, Paul McGrath and Andy Townsend. Nigel was a good lad to have around because of his good habits. He eventually left to join West Brom only because it was beneficial to him.

Like Nigel, Steve and Andy are also players of good habits. Paul is slightly different in as much that he is unable to do the same training as the rest of the players because of his knees. But he is not the sort I have to keep getting on to, apart from reminding him about wearing flip-flops. I have to say that when it comes to remembering that rule he is the worst. Otherwise he, Steve and Andy have never been a moment's problem to me. Nigel was the same before he moved on.

Steve was unfortunate last season because of so many injuries and, by his own admission, would say he was never really 100 per cent match fit. But he is still a superb and well-behaved individual. He is never late and is always well prepared for training and matches. He has always been spot on. The same can be said of Andy and Paul.

I am not suggesting that some of those who left were not in that category. They just did not suit the style of play I was trying to create. But the ones who remained have fitted the bill in terms of football and in terms of characters in the dressing room.

I think Andy had an exceptional season last season and, again, in the dressing room he is a remarkably funny person. He is the guy who comes out with the sharp one-liners. I don't hear some of them because he tends to be a bit quieter when I am around. But when the players are together I know he is as witty as any of them. He is arguably the senior professional at the club and very well thought of by the rest of the players. He comes to me with good ideas and is often the players' spokesman – not that he comes with an issue that often because every professional now knows how the club functions. But if anyone thinks I should be aware of the players' thoughts or ideas then Andy is the one who usually portrays it to me. He is a model professional, looking after himself off the field of play and an inspiration to his team mates on it.

Andy and Paul played a big part in our success of last season. Steve did not have much of an opportunity because of his injury problems, and, before he left us, Nigel was important on the sidelines and in the dressing room when it came to geeing up the players and getting them in the right frame of mind. He never tried to outshine Allan, John or myself but talked a lot of sense and was always urging the lads to do well. Michael Oakes, who took over the No. 2 goalkeeping spot when Nigel left, is still very young and fairly quiet. But he is an undoubted talent who will, not doubt, be pushing Bozzie all the way for a first team place.

Savo Milosevic was another fairly quiet guy last season. He tended to adopt the European life-style rather than get too much involved. For example, if the lads decided to go out for a few drinks after a match Savo would rarely be with them. That was not what he was used to playing in Yugoslavia.

It was a difficult first season for Savo because he was called away quite a number of times for international duty which meant an awful lot of travelling. But he is a very strong individual and needed to be because of a lot of unfair criticism he received. Perhaps he was punished because as a young lad he came into English football and boldly announced that he would score 25 goals in his first season with us.

That did not help him, and in his early days at Villa I pulled him aside and explained that the English media would be a lot different to what he had been used to back home. I explained that during the course of the season he would be asked awkward questions, so to try and learn that side of English football as quickly as possible. It is only when you sit down and talk to Savo, one-on-one, that you actually appreciate how well he has done to learn so much of the English language in such a short time. He no longer speaks broken English but puts sentences together very well and has worked extremely hard to master the language.

Soon after Savo arrived at the club one or two of the lads tried to wind him up in a friendly sort of way. For instance, Ian Taylor told him that the next time the manager spoke to him he had to reply with the words "Off you pop." Savo obviously thought Ian was teaching him to swear at me and was so reluctant to say anything. In the end he looked at me rather warily and whispered: "Off you pop," which had Ian falling about the dressing room with laughter.

Some of the lads also taught Savo to say to any player who walked in scruffily dressed: "The bins are round the back!" I did not mind things like that because he was not being told to swear or be nasty. It was just a bit of whole-hearted fun that helped the atmosphere in the dressing room. I am all for that kind of thing.

Some people would argue that I have steered clear of so-called high profile players to ensure harmony is maintained. I would counter that by pointing out that we finished fourth in the Premiership. I would add that, apart from Manchester United, my players were the only ones to win a major domestic competition last season. I also feel the best is yet to come, but I hope that in saying that they appreciate the fact that they still need a chief to bring the best out of them.

No matter how good they become they still need me to make the big decisions and to guide them in the right direction.

I mentioned what a happy lad Mark Draper is, but if you are looking for our 'double' act then you need look no further than Ian Taylor and Tommy Johnson. Ian just loves to be in where the action is, both on and off the field. If someone cracks a joke he is either part of it or leads the laughter afterwards. He has so much energy it is untrue, almost hyper-active. I think Ian enjoys every minute of his life at Villa. He and Tommy feed off each other and if I walk past the dressing room and hear laughter then it is a fair bet one of those two is behind it.

Tommy loves to exaggerate his Geordie roots which is great fun for me because of my upbringing. He has made sure he has kept his accent and loves to talk about the North East. He often has a quiet word with me claiming that I am 'a bit posh' now. Tommy is very well thought of in the dressing room, because of his openness and honesty more than anything else. I gave him freedom on the pitch and it took him some while to get used to the idea that I did not regard him as an out-and-out striker who played with his back to goal. He had convinced himself that he had to play up front but I think he has now even convinced himself that he is a better player coming from deep and running at defenders.

It is perhaps ironic that Ian and Tommy are the best of mates, yet they were the two invariably vying for one position in the team for much of last season. The fact that two guys trying to knock each other out of the side can get on so well with one another is brilliant for me. Again it creates that 'togetherness'. New rules allow us to have five substitutes on the bench this season and I believe that will help our situation by keeping the squad spirit going even more.

Players who are earning good money obviously like to spend some of it on clothes and that is another area where there seems to be quite a lot of mickey-taking in the more relaxed moments in the dressing room. Sometimes when I walk in I see that someone's clothes have been hung on a coat hanger from the ceiling, because they have been voted 'Clothes of the Day'.

To be honest, I cannot work out these days which are the designer clothes and which are not. It was far easier when I was a player. I have already mentioned the flared trousers and kipper ties, not to forget the platform shoes!

Sometimes I make sure I keep my finger on the button by insisting everyone turns up on a match day in blazers and flannels. It does not go down too well because it is not what most of them want. But at least they all look smart and well presented and there is no harm in that. But, overall, dress sense creates quite a bit of humour around the place, which is never a bad thing provided it comes at the right time.

There was certainly no place for humour in the dressing room the night Gary Charles suffered his unfortunate broken ankle injury towards the end of last season. Sometimes you do not realise how good a guy is until he is not there. I think that can be said of Gary without any fear of contradiction. I would describe him as an excellent full back but at the same time a fairly quiet guy, and even a little bit grumpy sometimes. Normally, during matches he would find himself operating down the entire right side and we would always be getting on to him to try to do that little bit extra. Often it got to the point where he would look over at the dug-out and say: 'Just leave me alone, will you!'

He perhaps thought we were being too critical but, in fact, all we were trying to do was encourage him. I would often shout back: 'It is no good moaning at me. I'm on your side because I think you are doing a great job'. But sometimes Gary did not see it that way. However, in our staff get-togethers it was often said that Gary was as good a team player as we had on the books. He picked up the sort of injury that you would not wish on anyone. It was horrible – that is the only way to describe it. In a way it killed off our season. Deep down we knew we did not need to do too much in the last three or four games, but once Gary suffered his injury I think all the lads would have been quite happy to finish the season there and then.

I remember watching Gary when he was with Derby County and thinking to myself that people did not realise just how classy he was. If anyone cares to watch a video of our goals last season they will probably be surprised to see how many times he was involved in the build-ups. Sometimes it may not have been the final pass but there were so many occasions when he had a part to play at some stage. He played a very big part in our successes of last season and will take a lot of replacing. Naturally, everyone would like to wish him all the very best for a speedy and full recovery. Hopefully, we will see him back playing again sooner, rather than later.

Our other attacking full back, Alan Wright, is often the victim of a bit of mickey-taking because of his size. If ever we have to be measured for new club suits or track suits you can see Alan begin to cringe because he knows that when the trousers arrive they will still need taking up a bit. Sometimes I have told the lad to turn up for a function in certain clothes, but Alan has had to arrive in something else because his wife has not had time to alter the trousers. Alan is a clever little fella, someone I would describe as a shrewd cookie. He is the type who sits behind big Paul McGrath and just lets the ribbing deflect over him. As the season progressed he began to throw in his two pennyworth. Alan might be a quiet lad but he is very reliable and tremendously well thought of in the dressing room.

Inevitably, after the European Championships Gareth Southgate became a topic of conversation for many people. Because of his nature and just the way he is Gareth is one of those guys who tends to have responsibility piled on him. All the good habits that I have talked about extensively are all second nature to him. But because of that I argue that there is no need to keep pushing things in his direction. Just because he is such a reliable, sound person, does not mean that I am going to put him under any unnecessary pressure.

Some managers might take the other option and increase his work load, on and off the field. But from a personal point of view I demand more of other people, maybe with the hope that they will be able to reach his standards. Perhaps in his early days as a professional Gareth was given the captaincy or asked to represent the players because he was so good at doing it. But I genuinely believe that one of the reasons why he had such a fantastic year for us last season was because it was a weight off his shoulders to have less responsibility. He could get on with his game rather than worry about the captaincy or organisation. He was allowed to be just one of the lads in the dressing room and he thrived on it.

He will always have the mickey taken out of him a bit by the other lads because he is so reliable. For example, if we go on trips abroad I invariably ask the players to bring their passports into work on the Wednesday, even though we do not really need them until the Friday. But you can guarantee that Gareth will be there on the Wednesday, passport in hand as requested. Although his approach is always spot on, he is another guy who likes a laugh and a joke. He likes being where the fun is and if the lads decide to have a night out he will be there with them. The fact that he is a smashing fella does not mean that he doesn't know how to enjoy himself.

A lot has been made of his penalty miss for England against Germany. Here was a lad who enjoyed an incredible season for us and, most of the time, was truly magnificent. Everything that could go right went right for him until his very last kick of the season. I know how disappointed he was at missing the penalty at Wembley but I am sure that one kick will not affect him as a player. I spoke to him on the telephone a couple of days after the Germany game and he assured me that although he was still a bit down he would be fine.

I told him I thought he had played brilliantly throughout the tournament and insisted that he had an extra week off before returning for pre-season training. I am never normally the sort to give people time off, but I felt Gareth was the exception to the rule and thoroughly deserved it. If you analyse his season and realise he kicked one ball wrong throughout the whole of it, then I do not think there can be too many complaints.

I suppose if you were looking for the 'Magnus Magnusson' of the dressing room it would have to be Ugo Ehiogu because he asks me and my staff more questions than the rest of the players put together.

People might ask why he is so quizzical. The answer to that is simple. It is because he wants to be good. He strives to be even the best. Often he will ask Allan Evans about how he played in the game that had just gone, or how he should approach the next one against a certain opponent. It does not worry me that Ugo turns to Allan rather to me to talk about defending. Many of you will remember Allan as a tough central defender who helped Villa win the League title and European Cup, so I cannot have too many arguments.

But it does not stop there. Ugo asks me about other aspects of the game. He will turn to Paul Barron to find out more about the diet he should stick to, or he will ask physio Jim Walker about any little knocks and bruises he might pick up which other players might not even bother to mention. When anyone watches one of our matches he probably does not realise just how well-prepared Ugo is. The lad wants to be a player in every sense of the word.

At every club I have been to there is always someone who wants something that bit different and Ugo definitely falls into that category at Villa. For example, if he fancies something different for a pre-match meal which he feels will do him good then he goes for it. It can often be a real pain in the backside for us because all the meals are ordered well in advance, only for Ugo to change his mind at the last minute. That is his little quirk and although it often leaves Allan, John and Paul tearing their hair out, he usually gets his way. In truth' it is only because he wants to learn and wants to be something special on the pitch.

There are one or two players I have not mentioned and that is nothing against them. Overall I just wanted to give everyone an insight into the way the dressing room operates, both during training and on match days. Maybe a few supporters will look at some of the players in a different light from now on having been told about some of their mannerisms, habits and quirks. But the bottom line is that I am very happy with the bunch of players I have around me.

Chapter Thirteen

Deadline Day

When dealing with the Press I am often asked if I can meet them at a certain time to ensure they beat their deadlines. Now as I reach the final chapter of this book I appreciate a little more what deadlines are all about.

We are just over a week into our pre-season training and the £1.5m signing of Fernando Nelson from Sporting Lisbon was completed a short time ago. But this is as far as I can go for the time being, except for saying that the real beat-the-deadline drama came just a couple of days ago when Dwight Yorke agreed to sign a new four-year contract with Aston Villa.

When you know that one of your best players has only a year of his current contract remaining, naturally, you want to do something about it as quickly as possible. Throughout last season Dwight played exceptionally well and although there were times when I wanted to begin negotiations on a new deal I felt it could become a distraction, and that was the last thing I needed.

If there was a criticism of Dwight when I first came to the club it was the fact that he did not produce his best form every game. But last season he was totally focused and that is how I wanted it to stay. So, although I mentioned it to him a couple of times in passing, I decided it was best to wait until the end of the season before beginning the serious discussions.

During May we established some common ground in as much that he intimated he wanted to stay with us and he knew that the chairman and I wanted him to remain. Initially, Dwight was talking about just a one-year extension on his contract and then, maybe, negotiate again in 12 months time.

But that was not an ideal situation for us. I had received a number of calls from a couple of leading European clubs asking me about Dwight's availability. I can also confirm reports that senior representatives from a top Italian club actually flew to England and came to Villa Park to meet the chairman and myself. It is one thing to receive phone calls and faxes enquiring about a player, but when they actually turn up on your doorstep you know they mean business.

They were very friendly discussions and the Italians even suggested that if they could not sign Dwight immediately, perhaps we would be interested in tying up a deal for the future. In other words they were quite prepared to let us keep him until his contract ran out next summer and then he would move to Italy.

We did not want any such thing to happen but as we also had calls from Spain as well we appreciated that we were dealing with an extremely hot piece of footballing property.

We made it very clear that we would not consider selling Dwight and discouraged both the Italians and the Spaniards from tabling a firm offer. We were even prepared to run the risk of keeping Dwight for the remaining year of his contract, even if he was not prepared to sign a new one.

Fortunately, when Dwight and his adviser sat around the table with the chairman and myself we were able to negotiate a contract which will keep the player with us until at least the year 2000. We were delighted Dwight pledged his future to Villa and I am sure all our supporters will look forward to seeing many more excellent performances and goals in the seasons to come.

I managed to have a few weeks' holiday during the summer which I believe is very important. I spend a lot of time wrapped up in my job and some of the people I work with often tell me I should get away from it a little more often. But even in the summer I find it difficult to relax because that is the time when a lot of ground work is carried out for the following season. This summer has been slightly different in as much that I have put this book together with my 'ghost writer' and I hope it has given you a bit of an insight into my life over the last 20 months or so.

Some of you will no doubt have noticed that during the past few weeks we not only signed Nelson and completed the Yorke deal but also negotiated new long-term contracts for Alan Wright, Ian Taylor and young Lee Hendrie.

When you read a line in a newspaper that new deals have been agreed maybe some of you think they took a couple of hours to negotiate. Nothing could be further from the truth. For example, Alan put pen to paper on a new four-year contract in June, yet discussions between his adviser and I began as long ago as last October.

During that time we had anything up to 10 meetings where we pieced together the contract details, such as rewards based on how much progress Alan has made during his time with us, and incentives for him to maintain the progress. This has become a very important phase in football as far as contracts are concerned, mainly because of the Bosman ruling. Chairmen and managers do not want players to be out of contract for fear of losing them on free transfers. Players appreciate that sometimes they may be better off by being out of contract, but that is the last thing a club wants.

So when Alan's new deal became public knowledge it was not just a case of sticking a piece of paper in front of him and asking him to sign it. From my point of view it gave me great satisfaction to negotiate deals with Dwight, Alan, Ian and Lee, knowing that they are happy to commit themselves to Aston Villa for at least the next four years.

There has also been the pleasure of rewarding young professionals with new contracts. Basically, it meant that every player in last season's youth team was given the opportunity to sign full professional terms. That must have been particularly satisfying for youth team coach, Tony McAndrew, who worked extremely hard with the youngsters and can now see the reward for his efforts. It was also pleasing for me because it meant that I did not have to sit a young player down and tell him that, unfortunately, he had not progressed to the standard required. On top of that several of the first year professionals earned a second year, once more underlining the strong base that has been built at the club in a relatively short space of time.

So, in fact, my 'quiet summer' was spent sorting out as many as 16 new contracts which proved very time consuming but well worth the effort.

I managed to work out deals which should mean us having a squad of players who, hopefully, will remain together for the next two to three years, at least, and maybe even longer. The nucleus is there and I would like to think that all that is needed for the time being is a bit of fine tuning.

Everyone was aware that the injury to Gary Charles meant I had to look for a new right back and I was delighted when I managed to sign Fernando Nelson, again on a four-year contract. Nelson, as he likes to be called, is only 24 but has already been heavily involved with the Portuguese squad. He has youth and under-19 caps and played no fewer than 23 times for the under-21 team. I regard him as a tremendous prospect to add to our squad and I am sure he will soon be adding to his five full international caps.

Now I have had time to sit down and reflect on the signing I am pleased to say I have managed to acquire the player who was my first choice. As ever, it was quite a complicated deal to negotiate although I had to smile when some of the newspapers referred to it as an ongoing saga. In effect, the transfer took just two weeks to complete, which is a very short time when you recall Alan Wright's contract took the best part of seven months to put together.

As far as I was concerned it was an absolute dream to get the Nelson deal tied up so quickly. I talked about it taking a fortnight but out of that time he was on holiday for seven days and I was on holiday for three days. So, in reality, all the negotiations with the agents and Sporting Lisbon took little more than three days to complete, which is quite unbelievable in this day and age. Nelson always had it in his mind to come and play in English football and was delighted when we moved in to sign him.

The new system of transfer deals certainly makes life easier when it comes to signing players from abroad. You may recall I detailed earlier how the chairman and I had to jump on an plane to Belgrade to negotiate the Savo Milosevic transfer deal. As far as Nelson was concerned we informed a licensed agent that we were interested in the player and the agent set the whole deal in motion enabling us to talk to Nelson and his club. At the end of it all Nelson, the agent and I met in the chairman's office at Villa Park for a meeting which lasted no more than about 45 minutes.

At the Press conference, called when we signed Nelson, I was asked if there were likely to be any more summer signings. The chairman made it clear that he would try to find the money if I needed to bring in another player, although I suggested that I had no one particular in mind.

For the first time I can now reveal that I was putting up something of a smoke screen over another deal. By the time you are reading this there may have already been another addition to my squad. Just in case there is not, I am not prepared to reveal any name.

But I can assure everyone that at the time of writing in mid-July there was someone I was trying very hard to sign. I have asked about the availability of the player and at this moment in time his manager does not want to sell him. But when I know who I want I find it very difficult to make do with a second choice. Sometimes I am prepared to wait to get my man.

If the deal goes ahead then it will be quite an expensive one. The chairman is aware of my feelings that the acquisition of this one player will make my squad complete. I am sorry if it all sounds a bit cloak-and-dagger, and the deal may or may not have taken place. Only time will tell.

Again, at the time of writing, I have had a little bit of criticism through letters in the local newspapers suggesting that I have not done enough business in the transfer market this summer. However, I would point out that the same thing can also be said of Liverpool and Arsenal, to mention just two clubs.

Their managers are obviously looking at their respective Premiership placings of last season and are aware that if they can turn a couple of results round, here and there, then they are capable of being up there challenging for the title, a major cup or a place in

Europe. As a result they are not buying players just for the sake of it. Most of the summer business so far has been done by clubs who did not have a particularly successful time last season and are eager to improve their League placing this time around.

I feel I have a group of around 20 players capable of doing very well for me and making us every bit as competitive as we were last season, hopefully even more so. I believe the experiences of the last two seasons – when we only just avoided relegation, then finished fourth in the Premiership and won the Coca-Cola Cup – will hold a lot of the players in good stead for the future. But they are all aware that success does not just happen. There has to be a lot of hard work and early indications suggest every one of them is prepared to put in the that work necessary to maintain the momentum.

Included in my first team group are the likes of young Lee Hendrie and Gareth Farrelly. Gareth has made big strides by becoming a full international for the Republic of Ireland. Both he and Lee, along with several other youngsters, will be looking to establish themselves as first team regulars.

The return after injury of Steve Staunton, Carl Tiler and Phil King will make competition for places even keener. That is almost like having three new players added to my squad. They know they will have to work their socks off to get into the team. But, by the same token, the players already in possession of a senior shirt know there can be no room for complacency with others breathing down their necks.

I have to say that there may be a couple of first team fringe players leaving us in the near future. If a player with a certain amount of experience is not a regular in the senior side then it might be better for him to move on. But, once more, only time will tell.

One disappointment in the summer was the decision by young Paul Browne to leave us and join Scottish club Raith Rovers. Paul played a couple of first team games towards the end of last season, and in June we offered him a new two-year contract. He came into my office to see me and actually shook my hand on the agreement.

As I have said, contracts can take some time to put together and I anticipated Paul would be signing once it was ready inside a few days.

However, he told me that he was going off on holiday but would be back in to see me as soon as he returned.

As a result of that conversation it came as a bit of a surprise when I received a telephone call from Raith a couple of weeks later saying they would like to sign Paul. On the same day I received a letter from Paul indicating that felt he needed regular first team football and had decided to move to Raith rather than take up our offer. I could see his point of view, to a degree, because he would struggle to get into our team regularly at the moment. But the fact that Raith only offered £50,000 for someone who had already played in the Premiership proved a bit disappointing to me.

We told Raith we expected them to make a decent offer for a player who has already appeared in the Premiership and potentially has a very good career ahead of him. But because of their reluctance to do so it meant that, at the time of writing, I was awaiting my first transfer tribunal as Villa manager.

I have been to several in my previous managerial roles. Normally, when you come out of them you say to yourself and the other club that it would have been much easier to reach agreement in the first place. I have no hesitation in wishing Paul all the best for the future, but I wish he would have come down and met me face to face to inform me of his decision, rather than drop a letter in the post.

The other hearings I had to endure at Leicester were disciplinary ones. Although I was never once booked as a professional player I had to attend an FA disciplinary hearing three years running at Leicester because of the poor record when it came to bookings and sendings off. Fortunately that has not been the case at Villa. Our record has been very good so far and last season we finished near the top of the Premiership Fair Play League, which was very pleasing. I think that underlines that the quality of the defenders we inherited and have brought in is very high.

Naturally, our defenders will have to be on their mettle and best behaviour as we look forward to playing in Europe in the new season. Winning the Coca-Cola Cup assured us of a place in the UEFA Cup at a comparatively early stage of last season. As it happened we would still have qualified for Europe through our Premiership placing, so that was doubly satisfying. I am sure everyone is looking forward as much as I am to being back in Europe.

My last European game as a player was in Barcelona's Nou Camp Stadium where we lost a UEFA Cup match after drawing the first leg 2-2 at home. That was the night my old pal, John Gidman, was sent off. Dismissals apart, European nights can be great occasions, as anyone who watched Villa win the European Cup against Bayern Munich in Rotterdam 14 years ago will testify.

I was recently looking through the list of teams in the UEFA cup this season and the quality is quite unbelievable. I believe it is now the toughest of the three European competitions to win, but we shall be doing our best to progress as far as possible. At the time of writing we were all anxiously awaiting the first round draw.

Overall, it promises to be another exciting season and one that the players, coaching staff and I are looking forward to enormously. We had a taste of success last season and we do not want it to end there. We shall be working very hard to keep the bandwagon rolling. We received tremendous support from our fans last season and with that kind of backing again I am sure it will go a long way towards helping our cause.

I hope you have enjoyed reading this book as much as I have enjoyed putting it together. I would like to think you know a bit more about my players, coaches and myself and the general running of a big football club like Aston Villa. We are all totally committed to bringing more honours to Villa and we hope we shall be giving you plenty to cheer about in the future.

RETURN OF THE LITTLE VILLAN

Chapter Fourteen

Transfers In

- Savo Milosevic ....Partizan Belgrade £3,500,000
- Mark Draper ....Leicester City £3,250,000
- Gareth Southgate .....Crystal Palace £2,250,000
- Tommy Johnson .....Derby County £1,900,000
- Julian Joachim ....Leicester City £1,500,000
- Fernando Nelson .....Sporting Lisbon £1,500,000
- Ian Taylor ....Sheffield Wednesday £1,000,000
- Alan Wright ....Blackburn Rovers £900,000
- Gary Charles ....Derby County £900,000
- Carl Tiler ....Nottingham Forest £750,000
- Franz Carr ....Leicester City £150,000

During the past 20 months I have negotiated new contracts with:

Dwight Yorke
Paul McGrath
Andy Townsend
Ugo Ehiogu
Alan Wright
Ian Taylor
Riccardo Scimeca
Michael Oakes
Stuart Brock
Neil Davis

Scott Murray
Gareth Farrelly
Lee Hendrie
Richard Walker
Darren Byfield
Ben Petty
Leslie Hines
Lee Burchell
Alan Kirby
Alan Lee

David Hughes
Lee Collins
Jonathan Miley
Richard Burgess
Adam Rachel
Darren Middleton
Aaron Lescott
Tommy Jaczszun

Transfers Out

- Earl Barrett .... .Everton £1,800,000
- Dean Saunders .... .Galatasaray £1,500,000
- Graham Fenton ...... .Blackburn Rovers £1,500,000
- John Fashanu .... .retired, compensation £1,000,000
- Guy Whittingham ..... .Sheffield Wednesday £700,000
- Garry Parker .... .Leicester City £650,000
- Dalian Atkinson ..... .Fenerbahçe £600,000
- Shaun Teale .... .Tranmere Rovers £500,000
- Kevin Richardson ..... .Coventry City £300,000
- Ray Houghton .... .Crystal Palace £300,000
- Chris Boden .... .Derby County £175,000
- Steve Cowe .... .Swindon Town £100,000
- David Farrell .... .Wycombe Wanderers £100,000
- Trevor Berry .... .Rotherham United £30,000
- Paul Browne .... .Raith Rovers .... .tribunal
- Nigel Spink .... .West Bromwich Albion .... .free
- Bryan Small .... .Bolton Wanderers .... .free

The following players were also released:

Dennis Pearce	Jamie Impey	David Moore
Ian Brown	Nii Lamptey	John Murphy
Darren Evans	Andy Mitchell	Danny West

Chapter Fifteen

The Manager and the Player

Brian Little was born in Newcastle upon Tyne on November 25, 1953. He played football for Seaham District Boys and East Durham Boys, before leaving school at 15 to join Aston Villa as an apprentice professional in 1969.

He turned professional two years later and made his first team debut as substitute against Blackburn Rovers in October of that year. In the same season he helped Villa beat Liverpool to win the FA Youth Cup. At the end of that season Brian played for England Youth in the Little World Cup in Spain, and picked up a winners' medal after helping beat West Germany in the Final.

Brian was part of the Villa team that won the League Cup in 1975 against Norwich City and again, two seasons later, when he scored twice to help overcome Everton in a second replay at Old Trafford.

His only England cap came in May 1975 when he appeared as substitute in the international against Wales at Wembley. Although he was only on the pitch for the final 10 minutes he had the satisfaction of laying on England's second goal for David Johnson.

During the 1979-80 season a proposed £600,000 move to Birmingham City fell through because of a back problem. But it was a severe knee injury which prematurely ended his playing career at the end of the 1980-81 campaign.

Brian made 301 first team appearances for Villa, including seven as substitute, and scored 82 goals. He was never booked during his professional career.

After Brian Little was forced to end his playing career through injury he spent three months working for a printing company. He then returned to Aston Villa and worked for eight months in the promotions department before being appointed youth team coach at the beginning of the 1982-83 season.

He stayed at Villa until the middle of the 1984-85 season before leaving to become first team coach under Sammy Chapman at Wolves. Following Chapman's departure at Molineux, Brian was appointed caretaker manager. But after only nine matches in charge he was sacked in October 1985 so that Graham Turner could take over the reins at Wolves.

Two months later, in December 1985, Brian joined Middlesbrough as youth and reserve team coach, serving under his former Villa colleague Bruce Rioch. He walked out of Ayresome Park in February 1988 and a few weeks later became Darlington manager.

Although Darlington were relegated to the GM Conference at the end of the season, Brian remained in charge and brought them back into the Football League the following season. He stayed at Darlington until the summer of 1991 when he moved to Filbert Street as manager of Leicester City.

He led Leicester to three play-off finals at Wembley and it proved third time lucky as he masterminded the victory over East Midlands neighbours, Derby County, to lead them back into the Premiership.

Brian stayed at Leicester until November 1994 when he resigned. Within a few days was appointed the new manager of Aston Villa.